A DAD IS BORN

A DAD IS BORN

A Week-by-Week Guide
Preparing Your Heart, Mind,
& Soul for Fatherhood

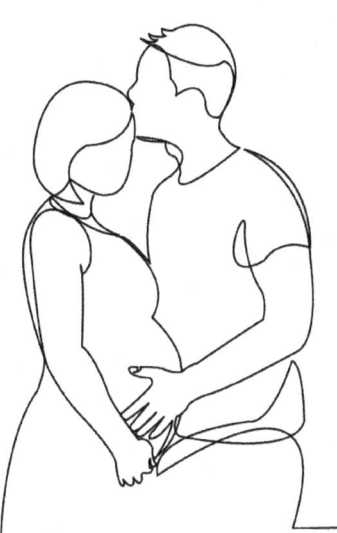

James R. Walters, Ed.D.

To my beloved wife and best friend, Suzie,
and my girls, Shea and Lily.
Thank you for transforming my heart and life.

Published in the United States by New City Press
136 Madison Avenue, Floors 5 & 6,
PMB #4290 New York, NY 10016
www.newcitypress.com
©2025 James R. Walters, Ed.D.

A Dad Is Born
A Week-by-Week Guide Preparing Your Heart,
Mind, & Soul for Fatherhood.

ISBN: 978-1-56548-720-8 (paper)
ISBN: 978-1-56548-721-5 (e-book)

Library of Congress Control Number: 2025934615

Printed in the United States of America

Contents

Introduction 7
    This Book's Conception..................................... 9
    Your Journey.. 13
    A Note About Language..................................... 16
    Let's Begin 17

This is Beautiful 18

First Trimester 22
    We are Having a Baby 22
    Doctor Visit.. 26
    Twelve Weeks Pregnant: Telling Family and Friends 29

Second Trimester.. 32
    Thirteen Weeks Pregnant: Fingerprints...................... 32
    Fourteen Weeks Pregnant: Soul Through the Eyes 35
    Fifteen Weeks Pregnant: Answered Prayers.................. 38
    Sixteen Weeks Pregnant: Listening Ears..................... 41
    Seventeen Weeks Pregnant: Another Miracle 44
    Eighteen Weeks Pregnant: Breathe.......................... 47
    Nineteen Weeks Pregnant: God's Direction.................. 50
    Twenty Weeks Pregnant: Snapshot.......................... 53
    Twenty-one Weeks Pregnant: Hairs on their Head........... 56
    Twenty-two Weeks Pregnant: Tears......................... 59
    Twenty-three Weeks Pregnant: Hope 62
    Twenty-four Weeks Pregnant: Assembly Required 65
    Twenty-five Weeks Pregnant: Play Ball...................... 68
    Twenty-six Weeks Pregnant: Falling in Love.................. 71
    Twenty-seven Weeks Pregnant: Within Yor Grasp 74
    Twenty-eight Weeks Pregnant: Dreams Come True.......... 77

Third Trimester 80
    Twenty-nine Weeks Pregnant: Just to See You Smile 80
    Thirty Weeks Pregnant: This Little Light 83
    Thirty-one Weeks Pregnant: Strength....................... 86
    Thirty-two Weeks Pregnant: What's In a Name 89
    Thirty-three Weeks Pregnant: Growing Stronger............ 92
    Thirty-four Weeks Pregnant: Finishing Touches.............. 95
    Thirty-five Weeks Pregnant: Love's Destiny 98
    Thirty-six Weeks Pregnant: These Things................... 101
    Thirty-seven Weeks Pregnant: This Season 104
    Thirty-eight Weeks Pregnant: Food for the Soul 107
    Thirty-nine Weeks Pregnant: Almost Time 110
    Forty Weeks Pregnant: Love 113

Your Baby is Born 116

Loss 119

Our Moms 125

Our Dads... 136

Conclusion 142

Notes.. 151

Sources Consulted... 154

Introduction

Congratulations! You are going to be a dad. If this is your first child, or if you are preparing to welcome another child into your fold, you already know that being a father is one of life's greatest gifts and responsibilities. This simple book invites you to pause weekly in prayer and focus your attention on the miraculous unfolding before you. Scripture tells us, "Seek ye first, the Kingdom of God" (Matt 6:13 KJV). These pages prepare your heart and mind to seek and discover God right in your home and heart.

As you likely know by now, this is a busy time, and as the anticipation increases with each week of pregnancy, so do your stress and responsibilities. These pages invite you to soak in this incredible season of transformation. Not only are mom and baby transforming, you too are going through your own metamorphosis. By the time you turn this book's last page, your child will be in your arms. I pray that, as you look back on this season of preparation, you will be overwhelmed with gratitude and a deeper love and appreciation for God, your own holy family, and the small village that lifts you up.

This book is structured in the following way. Each chapter is built upon a specific week of pregnancy, starting with when you find out that you are going to be a dad. The beginning of each chapter starts with a scriptural passage that connects to the week's theme. Then, there is a short description of what is happening inside the womb of the mother of your child. This will capture the precious moments of evolution and growth that prepare your child for entry into this beautiful world.

What follows is a brief reflection on the theme of the week that comes from my own experience and that of my fellow dads. While we recognize that each of us walks a different path, we also acknowledge much of what unites us in this holy vocation of fatherhood. I will summon spiritual words of wisdom from Catholic leaders who have paved the way before us. A short prayer based on the week's topic then follows for you to reflect on and recite. As the saying attributed to St. Vincent de Paul goes, "A man of prayer is capable of everything."

The chapter concludes with space for you to write a brief love note to your child. My hope is that many years from now, you will revisit these pages and be reminded of these earliest days of fatherhood. You may also choose, later in life, to share these reflections with your child. They will see a side of your love that may have been hidden or may not yet have been possible to comprehend. You are preparing a special gift for your beloved child.

This love letter is inspired by the wise and challenging advice of Mr. Joe Licata, a dear friend, teacher, and mentor, upon the birth of my first daughter, Shea. Here is his wisdom:

> At the end of each day, write a short note to your child. Some notes might be longer, recalling touching and inspiring moments from your perspective. On other nights, the note might be shorter, with a simple "I love you." On a special occasion, like their wedding day or milestone birthday, you may present them with a box filled with decades worth of those notes.

It would remind them, he said, "of the preciousness of their life, but most of all, share decades worth of the joy and love of their father."

To his incredible credit (he has seven children), from their very first day, he built a treasure chest of letters capturing the ordinary and extraordinary moments of their lives.

I tried this myself, and to be fully honest, as I strive to be throughout this book, it was a difficult task given the realities of balancing work, fatherhood, and being a husband (among many other vocations). I was more successful in writing "love notes" that I secretly inserted into the lunch boxes of my two children on school-day mornings. Shea, the sentimental type like her old man, has saved every note!

In this same spirit, see this book as a blank canvas, a free space to capture your thoughts and prayers from the very beginning of your child's life. It is the first chapter of what I pray is a classic, full of many, many more chapters of the love story between father and child.

The book is structured in a way that requires as little or as much time as you can afford. It is a weekly guide, and even if you miss or skip a week, you can easily revisit a chapter when time allows. This is all prayer, and there is no right or wrong way to proceed. It will serve as a gentle guide, reminding you to pause, to pray, and to look. Thank you for allowing me to accompany you on this journey. I hope that I, as a fellow dad on the journey, can offer insights that shift your perspective and ground your soul.

This Book's Conception

The origins of this book are a curvy and broken road that led to two other books before this very book was born. Like your own path to fatherhood, I share this here as inspiration and context.

In 2018, I was hard at work developing my first book, *Dreams Come True: Discovering God's Vision for Your Life* (published in May 2020). On a fateful bus ride in Northern Queens, New York, I felt great frustration with the writing process (as all creatives do) and was unsure if I could ever answer that relentless inner call to write a book that I prayed would make an impact for the better. I am not sure that anyone truly wants to write a book. It involves a monumental amount of work but also vulnerability and humility—all of which I would go to great lengths to learn and which would help me grow as an author and human being. Yet, somewhere, deep within, I felt a nudge to pursue this task relentlessly and faithfully.

At the time, I was reading a short book of reflections for the season of Advent inspired by the writings of one of my favorite authors, Henri Nouwen. I appreciated the book's structure of Scripture, reflection, and questions to consider during this liturgical season. As a fan of Christmas, I often looked at Advent as a necessary countdown to the big day. But that year, I was determined to delve further into this "purplish" season. As I stared out that Q46 bus window on Union Turnpike, a busy road in the middle of my beloved borough Queens, I wondered if Nouwen's book template could work for an altered message—this time for soon-to-be dads.

As I started to craft a first draft of this book for soon-to-be dads (while still developing *Dreams Come True*), I was also preparing for the arrival of a second child. Shea, my firstborn, took her first breath in 2006. Two years later, another baby was on the way. Having lived through a pregnancy already, I thought I was prepared to create a reflective resource for this miraculous journey from the father's perspective—using the same model as the Nouwen Advent book that rested in my hand.

The creative juices started to flow, and I used the opposite side of Nouwen's book's cover to draft a skeleton of an outline for the fatherhood book you are reading today. My writing stopped as the bus reached its destination, and I wouldn't revisit this idea until a few weeks later, when I was preparing a conference presentation in New Orleans, Louisiana.

A day prior to a presentation to a faith-based higher education community, I went to a local bar to watch the New Orleans Saints football game. With the Saints playing on the road, this was the next best thing, and as New Orleans scored quickly and often, before I knew it, the game became background noise. With a full belly and time to kill, I pulled out that familiar Nouwen Advent book that made the journey with me from the Big Apple to the Big Easy.

Suddenly, despite some appetizers and a few cold ones, I was stuck, like attempting to drive at 5 p.m. on a New York City highway. As a freshly poured beer arrived at my corner table, I wondered what would happen if there were no happy ending for future readers of this book. What if an expectant dad was stopped right in his tracks because the mother of his child suffered a miscarriage or delivered a stillborn baby? How would I make this work?

I struggled, as this wasn't something that I had experienced, and I felt guilty that I might be causing further harm. I was genuinely stuck, not sure if I wanted to contribute to what I imagined would already be a hell of a gut punch. As I chewed on this idea between the bites of stale nacho chips before me, I stopped writing, giving myself time to process this possibility before moving forward.

I could never have imagined, as I sat in that New Orleans bar on a Sunday afternoon, that only a few weeks later, on January 2, 2019, our first doctor's visit for pregnancy number two would change our lives, and I would soon understand how it felt to have hope turn into tears. When the doctor spoke the words, "This isn't a viable baby," I was devastated. I looked into my wife's eyes, and in an instant, I saw sadness and grief fill her face. I did everything in my power not to cry and vomit.

As many aspiring fathers know, the days and weeks that follow a miscarriage are incredibly tough, and the grieving process is difficult. It took about eight weeks to stop crying, not a coincidence, as this was the age of our baby when we found out her heart wasn't beating. I searched long and hard during those days for answers, and I made a commitment to write about it so future dads could find solidarity and eventually peace—something I desperately yearned for those days.

When I wrote my second book, *Batter Up: Answering the Call of Faith and Fatherhood* (published June 2022), I gave attention to miscarriages in one of its chapters, and I was moved by the many dads who shared with me their stories of sadness and loss. Words cannot take away the pain, but finding comfort in solidarity helps ease it.

The early drafts of *Batter Up* were developed as my newborn infant slept on my shoulder. I can recall, with mixed emotions, writing its early drafts, wondering what the future posed for our, hopefully, holy family. This infant, Lily, is our pandemic baby, born in May 2020. Living at the time in Queens, New York, we were at the epicenter of the world for the COVID-19 pandemic for several weeks. There were many nights when I wondered what the next day would bring as health never felt as precious as it did fragile. Charles Dickens famously wrote, "It was the best of times, it was the worst of times." Boy, did these words echo true.

The purpose of *Batter Up*, written during this time of uncertainty, was to celebrate fatherhood, combining the three areas of life that I loved the most: faith, fatherhood, and baseball. I smile as I recall those late nights and early mornings as my newborn's lips rested next to my ear, almost whispering the words I attempted to capture as I tried to craft a simple book about the extraordinary task of being a dad.

Fast forward to the fall of 2023, now with a seven-year-old and a three-year-old and just a few more well-earned wrinkles and grey hairs. I was driving home from a parent-teacher conference for the start of second grade for Shea and was moved by the presence of so many dads who cared about their kid's school, teachers, and faith. As I pulled over to fill the tank with gas, I remembered the book idea that I had not thought about since being in that bar in New Orleans almost four years prior—a guide for soon-to-be dads.

I cannot speak of the process for other writers and artists, but when I begin to feel inspiration, I cannot stop. I must put pen to paper, fingers to keys, paint to canvas. If I do not create, my spirit is blocked, and as I get older and, I hope, wiser, I recognize this as God working through me. All I need to do is cooperate and get out of the way. The same goes for fatherhood. Children do not come for us but through us, and it is our responsibility to God and to all of creation to nurture and love them so they can do the same for others.

The original idea for this book, first conceived on a city bus, took time to be born. Much would happen to better inform it. This included publishing two other books; the before-mentioned miscarriage; personal challenges with mental and physical health; job insecurity and new employment; the collective pain of a pandemic; loss of loved ones and changed relationships; increased global wars and suffering; the joys of bringing a second child into the world and raising her and her sister with my wife.

Your Journey

Like a child being created in a hidden darkness, so was this book. Fed by life's events and nurtured by God's grace, it is now time for this book to be born and to hopefully provide you comfort, guidance, and space to reflect and discern. You are likely reading this several weeks, if not months, into the pregnancy, and just as your baby is transitioning from a microscopic beginning into, soon, a bundle of joy, you are experiencing your own transformation.

I will attempt to capture some of those moments that inevitably occur during a pregnancy. This is informed not only by my own experience, but that of other dads who shared their stories with me. While the script isn't always the same, there are similar patterns and events that prepare us for fatherhood.

What is true for all of us on this path to fatherhood is the unique vocation we are called to by God. How and when we receive this call varies, but what unites us is that we do it together. Supported by God and loved ones, we enter this new reality. Soon, if not already, you realize that this is one of the most important roles you will ever assume. It is more important than the letters after your name, your job title, salary, bank account, brand of car, or the size of your home. It is why you are here. It is now who you are.

In my professional life, I am an author, human rights advocate, Catholic thought leader on fatherhood, pastoral minister, and organizational leader. These are some of the professional skills I have sharpened over the years. In my personal life, I am a son, brother, uncle, cousin, friend, husband, and yes, father.

To my children, I am a cook, cleaner, cuddle and tickle monster, artist, toy builder, athlete, taxi driver, joker, disk jockey, teacher, as well as many other roles I play throughout the day.

And of course, as a person of faith, I am (like you) God's beloved, a struggling-to-be-faithful servant who tries each day to reflect the divine love and peace that I receive daily. This relationship with God and others is not dependent on my actions, but on who I already am to God. When you hold your child, you will gain insight into how God loves us unconditionally. You will think, there is nothing this child could do that can change my love for them. Just imagine how God feels about us.

When I am operating out of this awareness that I call higher consciousness, I can see that of all my identities, it is first being God's beloved and second being a father that means the most. As much as you will be called to teach your child about God, they will teach you even more. The divine light that shines from them will not only transform your heart, but it will also deepen your own relationship with God and affect how you see life and your purpose in it.

Twentieth-century mystic Thomas Merton, in writing about the contemplative life, offers this insight that easily applies to the vocation of fatherhood and how you can choose to see yourself and your place in it:

> The Christian is then not simply a man of good will, who commits himself to a certain set of beliefs, who has a definite dogmatic conception of the universe, of man, and of man's reason for existing. He is not simply one who follows a moral code of brotherhood and benevolence with strong emphasis on certain rewards and punishments dealt out to the individual. Underlying Christianity is not simply a set of doctrines about God considered as dwelling remotely in heaven, and man struggling on earth, trying to appease a distant God by means of virtuous acts. On the contrary Christians themselves too often fail to realize that the infinite God is dwelling within them, so that He is in them and they are in Him. They remain unaware of the presence of the infinite source of being right in the midst of the world and of men. True Christian wisdom is therefore oriented to the experience of divine Light which is present in the world, the Light in whom all things are, and which is nevertheless unknown to the world because no mind can see or grasp its infinity.[1]

The same God who dwells within you now dwells within your child. They will remind you of this divine light daily if you recognize the divine amid the busyness, worry, and noise. For now, you find the divine in the mother of your child as she undergoes her own transformation. Her skin, if not already, will soon begin to radiate the divine light that reveals the miraculous.

The time will come when this book comes to an end, as will the pregnancy, and your child will enter the world. It is hard to describe that moment when you see your baby for the first time. My words don't seem to do it justice, but the best explanation I have found comes from Blessed Frederic Ozanam, the nineteenth-century founder of the St. Vincent de Paul Society, who says the following about the birth of his first child:

> My dear friend, one day you will experience the same emotion after several hours of terrible pains you hear the last cry of the mother and the first cry of the newborn child, then suddenly you see a tiny creature appear, that immortal creature of whom one becomes the guardian. At that moment something terrible and yet supremely sweet occurs in the depths of the soul, not in the metaphorical sense but in a real, physical sense. One feels as if the hand of God is remodeling one inwardly and shaping a new heart within.[2]

Yes, the hand of God is remodeling and shaping a new heart within you. Your life will never be the same, and you would never want it to be.

A Note About Language

I am sensitive to the fact that while many of life's roads lead to fatherhood, they do not all look the same. For this reason, I try to avoid assumptions as much as possible. For example, the mother of your child may not be your wife. She may be a girlfriend, a fiancé, or have another role. I will refer to her as mom, but I will avoid saying "wife" when not referencing my own beloved. If she is your wife, or whatever she may be to you and for you, feel free to interchange the appropriate word to make this as personal as possible.

Also, when it comes time to describe the baby, this book will differ from some other pregnancy books that refer to the baby by gender, using "he" or "she." I can recall reading a pregnancy book that used "he" as default. As I was having a daughter, it became a slight annoyance. For that reason, I avoid using "he" or "she" pronouns when referring to your baby. For consistency, I may simply write "your child (or baby)" or use the gender-neutral "them" or "they."

Let's Begin

Dad, you have been called to this most extraordinary and important role. Together, with help from above and within, let us prepare you for the transformation that has already begun.

This is Beautiful

St. Theophane the Recluse, a nineteenth-century Russian mystic, is to have said, "The concentration of attention in the heart—this is the starting point of prayer."

You likely have said a few prayers already since you heard you were going to be a dad. You may have even prayed years before in hopes of this responsibility and experience. This vocation or calling to fatherhood is a continuous prayer if we allow it to be. If we can live mindful of our God who works within us and within others, we will remain mindful of God's gentle hand guiding our steps, actions, and words.

At the heart of this vocation is beauty. Beauty is a word that carries deep spiritual meaning; it surpasses our society's superficial understanding of it, which often uses the term to label what is external and limited. As I write this book, I have a beloved wife of fourteen years and eight- and four-year-old daughters, and the most appropriate word to capture my life as husband and dad is beautiful. When I am operating as my best spiritual self, beauty is visible everywhere. My wide-opened eyes finally see what was always present. When I rest my eyes each night, knowing the ladies of the house are in their deep slumber, I think with a grateful heart, "This is beautiful."

From the sparkling eyes of the newly born to the wisdom-filled eyes of the dying, from the first flower bloom to the last falling leaf, beauty is always radiating. I am stopped in my tracks as I watch my wife comfort our crying daughter or spin her around the room, as Taylor Swift blasts from the speaker. Even the taste of our dinner, when my family surrounds the table, gains flavor and appreciation when

I stop and recognize what is occurring in that present moment. I invite you to search for beauty. It is here where we find God. It is always right in front of you. It just may require a shift in your perspective.

Our Catholic faith is rich in its exploration of beauty. The Pontifical Council for Culture, in its document *The Via Pulchritudinis: Pathway for Evangelization* (2006), wrote, "The *via pulchritudinis* [way of beauty] can open the pathway for the search for God."[3] Pope Benedict XVI recounts a story from his time as a Cardinal about a personal and profound experience he had with beauty. Along with an ecumenical group of clergy, he attended a Johann Sebastian Bach concert in Munich, which was conducted by the American Leonard Bernstein. The then Cardinal wrote of his impression: "Every expression of true beauty can thus be acknowledged as a path leading to an encounter with the Lord Jesus."

Your life and your family lead to an encounter with Jesus. Take a moment and reflect on this statement. Do you believe this? If you do, doesn't it change everything? In Pope Francis's apostolic exhortation *Evangelii Gaudium* (The Joy of the Gospel), the Holy Father writes, "Beauty is a key to the mystery and a call to transcendence. It is an invitation to savor life and to dream of the future."[4] These inspiring words echo the teaching from the book of Wisdom: "For from the greatness and beauty of created things comes a corresponding perception of their Creator" (Wis 13:5).

What makes beauty frightening is its fragility. I spent the early months of the lives of both of my daughters waking up to confirm they were still breathing. I feared the worst as they now were not only my responsibility but my everything. Nouwen writes this in his book, *With Burning Hearts*:

> The beauty and preciousness of life is intimately linked with its fragility and mortality. We can experience that every day—when we take a flower

in our hands, when we see a butterfly dance in the air, when we caress a little baby. Fragility and giftedness are both there, and our joy is connected with both.[5]

This fragility requires trust. Throughout the Bible, we read the words, "Be not afraid." This leads to a "yes," as the person on the receiving end of this directive proceeds with confidence and acceptance. We cannot ignore the fact that one day we will all return home to God. While we live this life, instead of fearing what could happen to end this beauty, we would make more of our time by allowing it to bring us closer to our Creator and to live with a joy that is God's free gift for us all to accept. Richard Rohr puts it this way:

> The good, the true, and the beautiful are always their own best argument for themselves, by themselves, and in themselves. Such beauty, or inner coherence, is a deep inner knowing that both evokes the soul and even pulls the soul into All Oneness. Incarnation is beauty, and beauty always needs to be incarnate, that is specific, concrete, particular. We need to experience very particular, soul-evoking goodness in order to be shaken into what many call "realization." It is often a momentary shock where you know you have been moved to a different plane of awareness. This is precisely how transformation differs from the mere acquiring of facts and information. Whereas information will often inflate the ego, transformation utterly humbles us. In that moment, we know how much *we have not known up to now, and still surely do not know*! This is a good and probably necessary starting place.[6]

Rohr writes of being shaken to experience a realization that moves us into a different place of awareness. If the news of your child didn't shake you, just wait until you hold that tiny baby in your trembling arms. Rohr is right in that fatherhood humbles you, and you soon learn that you don't even know what you don't know. Yet, there again is God. In your baby, your partner, the team of family and friends, and professionals who guide and support you as you say yes to being this baby's father. You will surely look in the mirror and wonder if you are ready. You will question everything and desire nothing other than your child's peace and joy. God is in your midst. So, remember that this is beautiful. Always.

In Nouwen's above quote, he writes that we can experience beauty and preciousness every day. Throughout these pages, as you look forward to the birth of your child, there is also a reminder to be present. Chiara Lubich, Foundress of the Focolare Movement, says the following:

> It is by living in the present that we can fulfill all our duties well.
> It is by living in the present that crosses become bearable: with good reason this practice is recommended for those who are nearing death.
> It is by living in the present that we can grasp God's inspirations, the impulses of his grace that come to us in the present. [...]
> So let's live the present moment! [...] Let us live it to perfection! In the evening of each day and in the evening of life we will find ourselves full of good works that have been accomplished and acts of love offered. ...[7]

First Trimester

Fathers are not born but made.
A man does not become a father simply by bringing a child into the world but by taking up the responsibility to care for that child. Whenever a man accepts responsibility for the life of another, in some way he becomes a father to that person.[8]

Pope Francis

We are Having a Baby

Scripture

> "For it was you who formed my inward parts; you knit me together in my mother's womb. I praise you, for I am fearfully and wonderfully made. Wonderful are your works; that I know very well. My frame was not hidden from you, when I was being made in secret, intricately woven in the depths of the earth. Your eyes beheld my unformed substance. In your book were written all the days that were formed for me, when none of them as yet existed" (Ps 139:13–16).

In the Mother's Womb

Mom won't even know she is pregnant until about six to eight weeks. Since fertilization, your baby moves from several hundred cells in week three to having a beating heart by week six. By week seven, your baby's eyes, nose, mouth, and ears are all beginning to take shape, and by week eight, fingers and toes miraculously begin to form.

In the Father's Heart

When my wife told me we were having a baby for the first time, shock quickly turned into fear. Suddenly, I worried about the size of our apartment, our bank account, and my inner ability to be a dad. I wonder if you have some of these same concerns.

As my baby was forming inside my wife, my own heart was beginning its own inner transformation. I waited and prayed for this moment, but I was, as my daughter now likes to say, "freaking out." Like others who embark on greatness, we must learn to trust God and know that we are playing a critical part in a much bigger plan. Trusting is never easy but remember that you are simply God's instrument. This saying is attributed to St. Francis de Sales:

> Do not fear what may happen tomorrow. The same loving Father who cares for you today will care for you tomorrow and every day. Either he will shield you from suffering, or he will give you unfailing strength to bear it. Be at peace, then, and put aside all anxious thoughts and imaginings.

Find peace in prayer, silence, and joy as you hold this secret with mom, knowing this adventure has only just started.

Prayer

Creator God, you formed me in my mother's womb and, since that day, prepared me for this moment. May I trust in you as I begin my own inner transformation as the earthly father of this new child who is beginning their story. Let us remember that you are with us as our new, holy family grows and as we begin this journey of pregnancy together.

✎ Love Note

Use the space below to write a short note to your child. (Recommendation: Reflect on how you felt when you found out that you were going to be a dad.)

_____
_____
_____
_____
_____
_____
_____
_____
_____
_____
_____
_____
_____
_____
_____
_____
_____
_____
_____
_____

Doctor Visit

Scripture

> "For surely I know the plans I have for you, says the Lord, plans for your welfare and not for harm, to give you a future with hope" (Jer 29:11).

In the Mother's Womb

As baby grows inside, mom will likely start to not feel well. For every mom it is different, but the first and third trimesters are often the most difficult. Although a home pregnancy test likely confirmed the pregnancy, a visit to the obstetrician (OB-GYN) will show you the first image of your baby. You may also hear the baby's heartbeat for the first time.*

In the Father's Heart

It is such a surreal moment. As the doctor uses a sonogram to reveal a black-and-white photo of your child, it is a real challenge to make out one end from the other (literally). The heartbeat, if it is strong enough, makes this experience a bit more real.

When you receive the parting gift of a sonogram printout, it is a hidden secret that you want to shout from the rooftops and go viral online. You may wait another few weeks before you share this news and bask in the joy and love of your communities. For now, hold your partner's hand and

---

* Fifteen percent of pregnancies end in miscarriage. If this is your experience, I am truly sorry. We experienced a miscarriage in my wife's second pregnancy. It was at this first OB-GYN appointment when we were told there was no heartbeat. Turn to page 119 for a chapter dedicated to this painful experience. If this isn't your experience, take time to pray for all those men and their partners who experienced or are experiencing this loss of a child.

thank God for this greatest of gifts. Trust in knowing that these simple words attributed to St. John Bosco echo true for your growing family: "God will provide."

Prayer

Lord, as I heard the heartbeat of my baby and saw their first image, it all suddenly felt real. I pray that my heart continues to be transformed to love my partner and child as you unconditionally love me. Thank you for the beauty of this experience.

📝 Love Note

Use the space below to write a short note to your child. (Recommendation: Reflect on hearing their heartbeat for the first time.)

Twelve Weeks Pregnant: Telling Family and Friends

Scripture

> "And he said to them, 'Go into all the world and proclaim the good news to the whole creation' " (Mark 16:15).

In the Mother's Womb

From weeks nine to eleven, your baby is starting to develop into the familiar image of a baby. By week eleven, they are kicking and stretching. By the twelfth week, you and mom might be ready to tell loved ones the good news. You may already have told a special few.

In the Father's Heart

It is quite a thrill to tell loved ones about your big news. When telling my parents about our first pregnancy, my mom screamed with excitement, and my dad wanted to go celebrate with dinner and drinks (unfortunately, no alcoholic drinks for my beloved wife).

When telling friends and colleagues, my soul was lifted by the sincere and genuine outpouring of love, prayers, and well wishes. So many joined us in anticipation. Make note of their smiles and their eyes filled with love—you will cherish those memories throughout your life. I learned quickly how this baby was not just our child but the newest member of our family and community, as we welcomed others into our web of love.

When we found out we were having Lily, our second child, there was great caution after the miscarriage. It was as if others tempered their excitement until we made it to this twelfth week. This caution only helps you appreciate the miracle and gift that is unfolding before you. I still rest my head some nights as they fall asleep, listening to their heartbeat and offering a prayer of gratitude.

Prayer

Lord, thank you for the gift of my family and friends, my companions on this journey of life. How blessed my child is to enter this world with so many who will care for them, continuing to reveal your unconditional love.

✏️ Love Note

Use the space below to write a short note to your child. (Recommendation: Recall some of the memorable reactions from loved ones as you shared this good news.)

Second Trimester

The heart of a father is a masterpiece of nature.

Attributed to Antoine François Prévost d'Exiles

Thirteen Weeks Pregnant: Fingerprints

Scripture

> "So God created humankind in his image, in the image of God he created them" (Gen 1:27).

In the Mother's Womb

The second trimester begins, and your baby is now almost three inches long. Your baby's organs are fully formed and continue to develop. On their small fingers, your baby has the beginning of their fingerprints, which will be fully formed by week twenty-five.

In the Father's Heart

Imagine the mark your child will leave on the world. You and close family members will be reminded of deceased and living loved ones by your child's features and mannerisms. Your baby will grow and find their way, discovering who God calls them to be for others. They will answer prayers with their kindness, intelligence, and love.

Imagine the injustices they will transform with peace. With your guidance and instruction, they will know right from wrong and learn how to empathize with life's complexities, accompany others on their journey, and, in the process, heal wounds. They will see suffering and respond with love. This is how they will leave their precious fingerprints on this world. Many years from now, when God calls them home, they will have left this life better than they found it.

You and mom will be their first teachers. Fill your mind and soul with wisdom and peace. Talk with mom about how you hope to raise your child. What will you teach them about how and when to pray, the importance of faith communities, and about service and charity, once they are old enough? What type of home will you create?

As you anticipate how your child will change the world, seek these words from St. Mother Teresa of Calcutta for yourself and reflect on your own contribution to making a difference in this one life: "Love begins at home."[9] Your children will be watching and listening.

Prayer

God, I do not know this child, yet I trust you have great plans for them. Help me instill in them a love for you, so they can be your instrument. Bless them and bless us as we transform into your little holy family.

✎ Love Note

Use the space below to write a short note to your child. (Recommendation: Reflect on some dreams you have for your child and what you hope for their life.)

Fourteen Weeks Pregnant: Soul Through the Eyes

Scripture

> "As it is written: What no eye has seen, what no ear has heard, and what no mind has conceived, the things that God has prepared for those who love him—These are the things God has revealed to us by his Spirit" (1 Cor 2:9–10).

In the Mother's Womb

Your baby's eyelids are fused over fully developed eyes. Your baby will also start to move their eyes.

In the Father's Heart

Just wait until your child's eyes lock with yours. Be prepared to melt as they look at you and see their dad. As the days turn into months and then into years, the connection will only deepen. They will learn how to make you surrender or negotiate more time for snuggles, books, or songs.

Their eyes will reveal the weight of their soul, their sorrows, and their joys. You will do all that you can to alleviate their pain and to celebrate their happiness. What a blessing it is to be on the receiving end of their glance.

There are some days, when I stare into my girls' blue eyes and I get lost. I am overcome by their beauty and their depth. I find a glimpse of God there, and a smile overtakes my aging face. It is as if God meets me there in all his beauty. Meister Eckhart writes about God's gaze this way:

There are of course millions of people and more but know that when God looks on one of them, alone, that one receives everything necessary from that singular gaze.[10]

That singular gaze from your child, revealing the indwelling of our Creator, is a gift. Soon you will understand, as those before you have but may have forgotten, as the seasons change and pass, and the noise distracts us from what is most innocent, pure, and real.

Prayer

As Jesus brought sight to the blind, help me see you in all my brothers and sisters. With anticipation, I wait to look into my baby's eyes. Until then and after, for all my days, keep open my eyes to your divine Spirit, present always in my midst.

✏️ Love Note

Use the space below to write a short note to your child. (Recommendation: Take time today and tomorrow and seek all the wonder of God's creation. Share what you saw and felt, so your child can learn and share this time of wonder with you.)

_____
_____
_____
_____
_____
_____
_____
_____
_____
_____
_____
_____
_____
_____
_____
_____
_____

Fifteen Weeks Pregnant: Answered Prayers

Scripture

> "For this child I prayed; and the Lord has granted me the petition that I made to him" (1 Sam 1:27).

In the Mother's Womb

Your baby is about the size of an apple, and they are now very active, rolling and flipping around their mother's womb. Mom may even begin to feel the baby move. Your baby's heart is pumping blood.

In the Father's Heart

When I was younger, I always hoped I would be a dad. Even though I was years away from meeting my wife, I had a deep knowing of what God was going to call me to do with my life. Having a wonderful father, and father figures surely contributed to this desire, but it is one of those rare and early understandings of why I am here.

I am not sure I ever specifically prayed to God for a child, but as I look back on my life, I can see how God was using my participation in this divine dance as preparation for fatherhood. All of my being led me to this place.

Dorothy Day writes, "You will know your vocation by the joy that it brings you. You will know. You will know when it's right."[11]

God knew what was on my heart, and God knows what is on your heart, too. When you hold your baby, and even now as you accompany and support mom, you too know that this vocation is your call to answer and claim.

You will soon realize that your life has been a prayer that has always led to this moment.

Prayer

Heavenly Father, you know what is on and in my heart, even when I lack the words. Provide me the grace and strength to trust in you, to answer your heavenly call with a resounding yes.

✏️ Love Note

Use the space below to write a short note to your child. (Recommendation: Share with your baby how God has prepared you and is currently forming you to be their dad.)

Sixteen Weeks Pregnant: Listening Ears

Scripture

"Let anyone with ears listen" (Matt 11:15).

In the Mother's Womb

Your baby's eyelids, upper lip, and ears have developed. They can hear you, so talk and sing to your child every moment you can!

In the Father's Heart

The first time I met my first child, Shea, she was in the neonatal intensive care unit (NICU). It was a few hours since she was born, and her mom was recovering in a separate room after a difficult and frightening delivery. As I walked down the hallway, only one child was screaming, and it was my baby girl. When I approached her tiny body, covered in tubes and beeping wires, I uttered these words, "You are so cute." In an instant, her crying stopped.

A nurse walked by and said, "She knows her daddy's voice." That was the first time someone called me by that name.

As you prepare for your child, talk to them. Tell them what is on your heart and sing those songs that lift your soul. When they grow older, their ears will welcome how you discuss God and the importance of faith. Your actions will speak louder than words, but your words will carry great weight. You will have to choose your words wisely as those words will form their inner thoughts and shape their worldview.

For now, do not worry about those future days. Embrace this time when your baby comes to know the voice of their father, who will point them to their Heavenly Father from now on.

Prayer

Lord God, help me to hear your voice. Continue to form me as your son, so I can be the father my child deserves. Guide me so I can guide my child to you.

✏️ Love Note

Use the space below to write a short note to your child, (Recommendation: Share the lyrics of a song that captures how you feel about them. Sing this song to them and make note of what it represents.)

_____
_____
_____
_____
_____
_____
_____
_____
_____
_____
_____
_____
_____
_____
_____
_____
_____
_____
_____

Seventeen Weeks Pregnant: Another Miracle

Scripture

> "Jesus said to them, 'Fill the jars with water.' And they filled them up to the brim. He said to them, 'Now draw some out, and take it to the chief steward.'
> So, they took it. When the steward tasted the water that had become wine and did not know where it came from (though the servants who had drawn the water knew), the steward called the bridegroom" (John 2:7–9).

In the Mother's Womb

Your baby starts to add fat to their body! Fat gives your baby energy and helps them stay warm after they are born. Your baby's taste buds are also starting to work, and they can even tell the difference between sweet and bitter.

In the Father's Heart

During the wedding at Cana, Jesus performs his first miracle by turning water into wine. It isn't just any ordinary wine, but a better wine than what was being served at the start of the festivities.

Your child is a miracle, and they will exceed all your hopes and desires. God is blessing you, your family, and the world with this gift. Celebrate what is happening right now in your baby's mother's womb. It is another miracle that we cannot take for granted.

The steward at Cana did not know where the new wine came from. But you know where your child comes from and who is responsible for sending this angel into your life.

Prayer

My Creator, you intercede in bringing life and joy into our lives. Bless our beautiful miracle, as they develop within their mother's womb, and bless them always, as they follow your path until they return home to you.

✎ Love Note

Use the space below to write a short note to your child. (Recommendation: Try to put into words how you are feeling as you [try to] process the miraculous.)

Eighteen Weeks Pregnant: Breathe

Scripture

> "The Spirit of God has made me, and the breath of the Almighty gives me life" (Job 33:4).

In the Mother's Womb

In your baby's lungs, the smallest tubes, known as bronchioles, are starting to develop. At the end of these tiny tubes, respiratory sacs begin to appear. When your baby is ready to be born, these sacs will be entangled with tiny blood vessels that allow oxygen and carbon dioxide to flow in and out.

In the Father's Heart

As your baby prepares to breathe, allow this to be time for you to breathe. There is no shortage of concerns to worry about, from money to living arrangements to, most importantly, the health of mom and baby. How are you finding time to take care of yourself?

Only after having two young children, job insecurity, and a global pandemic did I focus on my own mental health, specifically anxiety. I built a team of gentle experts who helped me learn, heal, and improve on the physical, spiritual, emotional, and psychological dimensions of my true self. I learned new skills and my perspective slowly changed. With the support of my wife and loved ones, I finally learned how to fill my own cup so I could better pour my love into others'. Build that team for yourself, no matter what challenges may exist. As men, we sometimes feel as if we must go about this alone or that we need to have all the answers and figure out all our challenges. Shift from this mentality to one of communion and an openness to allow others to serve and heal you. Henri Nouwen writes:

> Exhaustion, burnout, and depression are not signs that you are doing God's will. God is gentle and loving. God desires to give you a deep sense of safety in God's love. Once you have allowed yourself to experience that love fully, you will be better able to discern who you are being sent to in God's name.[12]

You are being sent, in God's name, to be a father. Taking care of yourself holistically is not only a gift to you but also a gift to others, especially to your holy family that depends on you and follows in your ways.

Prayer

God of peace, this is not easy. At times, I feel overwhelmed and even scared. I know who I am called to be and what to do, yet I struggle. Help me as I breathe, to be aware of your divine Spirit, and help me to trust in your guidance and love.

✎ Love Note

Use the space below to write a short note to your child. (Recommendation: Share with your child all that is in your heart. Not only will this allow you to process and heal, but it will also model for your child the importance of holistic health, and you will grant permission for them, when older, to be vulnerable and honest, and to seek support—including care from you.)

_____
_____
_____
_____
_____
_____
_____
_____
_____
_____
_____
_____
_____
_____
_____
_____
_____
_____

Nineteen Weeks Pregnant: God's Direction

Scripture

> "Strength and dignity are her clothing, and she laughs at the time to come. She opens her mouth with wisdom, and the teaching of kindness is on her tongue" (Prov 31:25–26).

In the Mother's Womb

Your baby is the size of a beef tomato, getting bigger and stronger by the day. Mom will really begin to feel your baby kicking and moving. Your baby also starts to suck their thumb, preparing for birth in just over four months.

In the Father's Heart

As mom starts to feel the baby kick, you will have to wait at least another five weeks before you will feel it from the outside of mom's belly. Take this time to be present and watch mom's face as she reacts to the stronger sensation. As they strengthen their bond, allow this to be a time to grow even deeper in your relationship with your partner. Marvel at how she is glowing, serving as a sacred vessel for your child.

This is an invitation to honor mom. St. Therese of Lisieux is credited with saying, "The loveliest masterpiece of the heart of God is the heart of a mother."

Find peace here this week. You probably know by now that pregnancy isn't a walk in the park, so find ways to make it easier on mom. The second trimester tends to be a little easier for most, as the morning sickness fades, and you are not yet faced with the uncomfortable realities of the third trimester. Enjoy this time together, go for walks, and celebrate every doctor visit. Allow this to be a season of preparation, as transformation is occurring for all of you.

Prayer

Mary, Mother of God, I call upon your intercession. Protect the mother of our baby. Comfort her during the trials of this pregnancy and keep her eyes on you and your Son. Thank you for this miracle in my midst, and help me to help them. (Recite three Hail Marys.)

✏️ Love Note

Use the space below to write a short note to your child. (Recommendation: Share something about their mom with your baby. Write about your love and appreciation for their mom and what internal and external qualities you hope your baby will inherit from their mama.)

_____
_____
_____
_____
_____
_____
_____
_____
_____
_____
_____
_____
_____
_____
_____
_____
_____
_____
_____
_____

Twenty Weeks Pregnant: Snapshot

Scripture

"For we walk by faith, not by sight" (2 Cor 5:7).

In the Mother's Womb

It is finally time; you will "see" your baby. As it was during your first visit, it may be hard to make out what you are looking at, but your doctor will help, and they will provide a printout to take home. This time, the image will better resemble your baby who you will meet in another twenty weeks. As you admire this image, you may find comfort in knowing your baby now goes to sleep and wakes up throughout the day. Mom's movements and loud noises can disturb their slumber.

In the Father's Heart

Some choose to find out the baby's sex at this point, while others wait for their grand arrival. Whatever you and your partner decide, there is an invitation to ponder:

- What will your child look like?
- What will you name them?
- How will you decorate their room?

These are just a few of the questions that you will ponder as you near the halfway point of the pregnancy.

As for my journey, this is when it started to feel most real. With our oldest, my wife surprised me with two onesies that revealed I was going to have a daddy's girl. I didn't have any rooting interest other than health, but I could feel my heart begin to mold and prepare for a little girl who would rely on her old man, knowing the pivotal role I would play in setting the bar high for how others would treat her. When we found out that our second was a girl, I couldn't have been more excited. I knew after three years with Shea that God was always preparing me to be blessed among women.

No matter their biological sex, your baby is and will forever be the love of your life. Read these words from an address Pope Francis gave on February 11, 2015, to a General Audience in St. Peter's Square:

> Children are loved before they are born. I often encounter expectant mothers in the square who ask me to bless their unborn babies. These children are loved before they come into the world. This is gratuitousness, this love; they are loved before they are born, like the love of God, who always loves us first. They are loved before having done anything to deserve it, before being able to speak or to think, even before being able to come into the world. To be sons and daughters is the fundamental condition for knowing God's love, which is the ultimate source of this authentic miracle.[13]

Prayer

God, how I love my baby who slowly is transforming within their mother's womb. I find gratitude in this moment, learning the depths of your love each day. Thank you for loving me into being and thank you for this most miraculous of gifts. I promise to love our child as you have loved me. Amen.

✏️ Love Note

Use the space below to write a short note to your child. (Recommendation: Describe the doctor's visit and what it felt like to see your child. If you found out their sex, share your reflections and hopes for your son or daughter.)

Twenty-one Weeks Pregnant: Hairs on Their Head

Scripture

"But even the hairs of your head are all counted. Do not be afraid, you are more value than many sparrows" (Luke 12:7).

In the Mother's Womb

Your baby's fingers and toes are fully formed. The baby is now the size of a carrot. They are also developing their hair and eyebrows.

In the Father's Heart

You are more than halfway to your baby's birth, and I can recall that this was the time when fear started to increase. The initial shock from the positive pregnancy test and early doctor visits gave way to caring for my wife and to the excitement of having a baby. Now, as the weeks increase and mom's stomach continues to grow, having a baby is becoming more real.

Trust that God not only knows the number of hairs on our head, as Jesus tells us, but God also knows the number of hairs on your child's head, however few there may be right now. Jesus reminds us to not be afraid. Easier said than done, but remember: This isn't a sweet suggestion but a gentle command so we can be fully present to the miracles before us.

St. Augustine is credited with saying, "God loves each of us as if there were only one of us." The God that loves us unconditionally and beyond our comprehension knows the number of hairs on your head and all the fears and dreams in your heart. Trust in the Lord.

Prayer

Let us quietly recite these beautiful words attributed to St. Thomas Aquinas: "Grant me, O Lord my God, a mind to know you, a heart to seek you, wisdom to find you, conduct pleasing to you, faithful perseverance in waiting for you, and a hope of finally embracing you." Amen.

✏️ Love Note

Use the space below to write a short note to your child. (Recommendation: Share your fears and your own challenges in trusting in God at this time).

_____
_____
_____
_____
_____
_____
_____
_____
_____
_____
_____
_____
_____
_____
_____
_____
_____
_____
_____
_____
_____
_____
_____

Twenty-two Weeks Pregnant: Tears

Scripture

> "He will wipe every tear from their eyes. Death will be no more; mourning and crying and pain will be no more, for the first things have passed away" (Rev 21:4).

In the Mother's Womb

Your baby's eyelids are still shut, but their eyes are moving behind them. Amazingly, their tear ducts start to develop.

In the Father's Heart

When your baby enters the world, they will cry. This is a glorious occurrence as your baby transitions from the womb to breathing in air for the first time. For many more days and nights, crying will be their best mode of communication. Each time, your heart will ache as you try to figure out how to end their tears, and quickly.

As they grow older, different tears will be shed, like when you leave them at school for the first time, when they have a conflict with a friend, and when they are struggling with academics or relationships. Tears will painfully flow when they lose a loved one to death, when their world crashes in on them, and when they inevitably battle, break, and heal along life's journey. There will also be tears of joy when they are overwhelmed with happiness—such as seeing you after a business trip or opening the perfect gift on Christmas morning.

You may be there to wipe the tears, but you may not be able to stop them. At times, all you can do is hand them a tissue and accompany them as they navigate the passing of a storm. We are reminded in faith that in the end, when this life's journey concludes for each of us, no more tears will be shed. This brings us consolation and hope, yet in the meantime, we prepare our hearts and spirit for what will be, for better and for worse.

Prayer

God of comfort, I know that my consolation is limited. I am grateful for you, and I rely on your wisdom to help me accompany others, especially my wife and children, when they are suffering and in pain. I cannot do this alone. Give me strength and comfort me, as I do my best to comfort others, especially my baby.

✏️ Love Note

Use the space below to write a short note to your child. (Recommendation: Share a time when tears flowed from your eyes and how someone comforted you. Provide encouragement that you will always be there for them, especially when they need you the most.)

_____
_____
_____
_____
_____
_____
_____
_____
_____
_____
_____
_____
_____
_____
_____
_____

Twenty-three Weeks Pregnant: Hope

Scripture

> "For surely I know the plans I have for you, says the Lord, plans for your welfare and not for harm, to give you a future with hope" (Jer 29:11).

In the Mother's Womb

At one pound, your baby is now the size of a large mango. Your baby's face is beginning to look a lot like it will when they make their grand debut in a few months.

In the Father's Heart

Mom is about five months pregnant by now, which means you have been accompanying them during their transformation. It is a great opportunity to pause and continue to recognize how God is transforming you. Poet Kahlil Gibran writes, "Your children are not your children. They are sons and daughters of life longing for itself. They come through you but not from you. And though they are with you yet they belong not to you."[14]

God is presenting you with an incredible responsibility, and like St. Joseph, we are charged to nurture, form, and love our child so they can fulfill God's great plans for them. Instead of feeling fearful, we should be filled with hope. Is there a greater honor and responsibility than to be this child's dad?

St. Peter Julian Eymard writes this of St. Joseph and his vocation:

Truly, I doubt not that the angels, wondering and adoring, came throning in countless multitudes to that poor workshop to admire the humility of him who guarded that dear and divine child, and labored at his carpenter's trade to support the son and the mother who were committed to his care.[15]

We trust that those same angels are among you and mom as you manifest God's plan that is fulfilled within you and your child.

Prayer

St. Joseph, I call upon your intercession to support my journey, and the journey of all dads, into the unknown. Help me replicate your strength, humility, and trust in God, so I may guide my child to come to know and love your son and our savior and friend.

✏️ Love Note

Use the space below to write a short note to your child. (Recommendation: Write a prayer to St. Joseph and share it with your child, if you are comfortable.)

Twenty-four Weeks Pregnant: Assembly Required

Scripture

> "For every house is built by someone, but the builder of all things is God" (Heb 3:4).

In the Mother's Womb

As your baby continues to grow, gain weight, and prepare for life on the outside, mom may also feel the need and instinct to prepare your home for the baby's arrival. Known as nesting, she may be focused on cleaning and ensuring that all is set for the little one. As the third trimester nears and simple tasks will grow in difficulty, this is an important time for mom and her peace of mind.

In the Father's Heart

There is so much still to do. And while there is plenty of time, you may be feeling the pressure of the world while building furniture, painting walls, and stocking up on diapers and onesies. I have a now wonderful memory of painting furniture while watching a baseball game in the background. With each brushstroke on the cabinet, I imagined the little clothes that would fill these drawers. I envisioned with excitement what this room would become and how a baby would soon fill the space. It became an act of love and service, as well as a challenge in developing a new skill.

There was other furniture to build, leading to an increase in prayers to St. Joseph. A changing table for my second child included over one hundred pieces that were mostly all used.

Ten hours later, with some prayers and expletives along the way, this act of love was more than just checking off another item from the to-do list; it was one step closer to creating a home for my baby.

Furniture is not the only self-assembly required as you are rebuilding yourself in anticipation of baby's arrival. In Proverbs 20:7, we read: "The righteous walk in integrity—happy are the children who follow them." How are you preparing yourself to be a father not only to your child but to your community?

Prayer

St. Joseph, I call upon your intercession again as I build not only the furniture and prepare the physical space for my child, but as I rebuild my heart for this vocation. Help me see the beauty in this time amidst the demands; help me to love and be present to the miracle before me.

✎ Love Note

Use the space below to write a short note to your child. (Recommendation: Share a story with your child about preparing their space, be it painting, assembling, or building. Share your excitement as their space is being constructed.)

_____
_____
_____
_____
_____
_____
_____
_____
_____
_____
_____
_____
_____
_____
_____
_____

Twenty-five Weeks Pregnant: Play Ball

Scripture

> "Train children in the right way, and when old, they will not stray" (Prov 22:6).

In the Mother's Womb

Your baby is now the size of a soccer ball, and they can now stick out their tongue. Their nose is also working, practicing breathing, and smelling scents in utero.

In the Father's Heart

Your baby is now the size of a soccer ball. In what will feel like a flash, you will be teaching your child how to kick a soccer ball, catch a baseball, dribble a basketball, throw a football, or join you in recreational activities that you enjoy.

When my oldest started playing tee ball, she just wanted to stand next to me on the infield dirt. It didn't matter if she caught the ball or threw it to the right base. I don't even think she really enjoyed it (soccer was more entertaining), but she amused her old man and hung around the baseball diamond for some special bonding time. My youngest, who benefited from watching her older sister play soccer for a few years, picked up the game quickly, easily dribbling the ball that was at first, half her size. There are so many wonderful Saturdays ahead of you when your little one will learn the games you love and, in time, reveal what their own passions are, which you, too, will learn to appreciate (if you don't already).

While soccer captures the heart of my girls, baseball is my favorite sport. Baseball teaches us a theme that is often present in all of our passions. I leave you with this touching quote from Richard Wagamese, who writes about baseball, that captures the beauty of sports and other collaborative efforts, and very much connects to our role as fathers: "I love the central metaphor of the (baseball) game—all of us helping each other to make it home. Funny how a game can teach us so much about life."[16]

Prayer

God of life, guide me as I prepare to be a father to this child. Allow me to live each day with the same passion I show for my sports teams, and help me as the great coaches do, to lift my child up and support them as they use their gifts and talents to serve you.

✎ Love Note

Use the space below to write a short note to your child. (Recommendation: Share a memory of playing a sport or recreational activity with your dad, grandfather, or uncle. What was that like and what do you remember? Write not about what you did but what you felt, then and now.)

Twenty-six Weeks Pregnant: Falling in Love

Scripture

> "...I pray that you may have the power to comprehend, with all the saints, what is the breadth and length and height and depth, and to know the love of Christ that surpasses knowledge, so that you may be filled with all the fullness of God" (Eph 3:17-19).

In the Mother's Womb

Your baby now weighs two pounds, and their eyes are beginning to open. When you and mom speak, baby will hear you and respond with changes to their movement, heartbeat, and breathing.

In the Father's Heart

Do you remember the first time you fell in love with baby's mom? Recall the sweaty palms, racing heartbeat, and butterflies in the stomach.

    I have such wonderful memories of anxiously walking to my then-girlfriend's apartment, feeling a rush of energy and joy to simply be in her presence. We started dating in the winter, so even to this day, when we kiss on a cold day, those butterflies come right back.

    Your baby is slowly falling in love with you and mom. They are physically reacting to your voices, and the best part is that it only gets better from here. Just wait for those cuddles! My two girls are still young, and older dads warn me of potentially tumultuous times when the teenage years arrive. Recently, a father of two daughters in their twenties, said to me, "The hugs will stop for a little while, but they come back."

For now, I cherish those little girls wanting to begin and end each day in my arms. Soon, you will too. Enjoy these early days when your love story is just beginning.

Prayer

God of love, I cannot even grasp your love for this baby and for mom. I cannot grasp the magnitude of your love for me. Thank you for welcoming my holy family into your fold. My heart, filled with gratitude, overflows.

Love Note

Use the space below to write a short note to your child. (Recommendation: Share a memory of what it is like to fall in love with them.)

Twenty-seven Weeks Pregnant: Within Your Grasp

Scripture

"With a strong hand and an outstretched arm, for his steadfast love endures forever" (Ps 136:12).

In the Mother's Womb

Your baby is the size of a head of cauliflower. They are very active (just ask mom), often stretching and making grasping motions with their tiny hands.

In the Father's Heart

Just wait for your baby's small fingers to grasp yours. As the weeks turn to months, your baby will desire to wrap themselves in your arms. As they begin to walk, they will reach for your support and safety. When you snuggle on the couch or in bed, they will wrap their hands around your neck and find peace there.

If you are both blessed, you will live long enough to grasp for them as you cautiously take a labored step or seek comfort in their familiar touch, as it is now you who will find rest in their strength. Together, you will spend your shared days reaching for God, attempting to capture his unlimited and unconditional love. You will teach one another what it means to be loved by your Creator and to be an instrument of that same love for each other and all in your company. For now, hold on to this moment, trusting in our God, as all this transformation continues. But keep your eyes on the prize, as what you seek you will soon hold in your arms and forever in your heart.

Prayer

At times, Lord, I fail to remember your love for me. Help me recall how you see me—as your beloved—and how you comforted me in times of trial and difficulty. As I look back at my life, I see your gentle hand lifting me up, nudging me forward, and holding me in tranquility. Allow me to reflect on this love now, in all my encounters, and soon, as I welcome our child into this precious world.

✍ Love Note

Use the space below to write a short note to your child. (Recommendation: Share a time when you reached for God, calling for God's grace and love during a moment of need or in a moment of immense joy.)

Twenty-eight Weeks Pregnant: Dreams Come True

Scripture

> "Commit your work to the Lord, and your plans will be established" (Prov 16:3).

In the Mother's Womb

Your baby begins to experience rapid eye movement (REM) sleep, which means it is likely that your kid is dreaming for the first time.

In the Father's Heart

Can you even imagine the dreams in your child's heart? Just imagine how God will call your child to be a light in the world.

You can be like the father of St. Francis of Assisi and dismiss your child's desire to love and serve as eccentric and even concerning, as it may be. You might also be like St. Thomas More, modeling for your children your love of God and the importance of integrity and faith.

Whomever your child is called to be, you have a choice: Will you support and guide them, or will you act out of your own fears and concern for what others might think, or give in to your own limited judgment and shortcomings?

Be their biggest fan and support, guiding your children to fulfill what God asks of them. And what God has asked of you is to be this child's father. G.K. Chesterton is credited with saying that "God chooses ordinary men for fatherhood to accomplish his extraordinary plan." Yes, this is extraordinary, it is beautiful, and it is beyond our imagination.

Prayer

God of unconditional love, I wonder who my child will be and if I can be the dad they need me to be to love and support them. Guide me to better trust in you and who you formed me to be. May I seek you always and find comfort and answers in your love.

Love Note

Use the space below to write a short note to your child. (Recommendation: Share a time when someone older supported you and helped you achieve your dreams.)

Third Trimester

Fathers have to be patient. So many times there is nothing that can be done but wait in patience, kindness, generosity, and mercy, and pray.[17]

Pope Francis

Twenty-nine Weeks Pregnant: Just to See You Smile

Scripture

"The Lord has done great things for us, and we rejoiced" (Ps 126:3).

In the Mother's Womb

Your baby is the size of a butternut squash. They are now smiling, most often when sleeping. Mom has been pregnant for seven months already, and the homestretch has officially begun.

In the Father's Heart

In 1997, country star Tim McGraw had a number-one hit with the song "Just to See You Smile."[18] While the song is about a significant other, it could easily be said when a dad looks at his child.

Just imagine those future moments when their smile will melt your heart. Just to see them smile will drive you to come home with a special treat from the bakery or place that long-wanted gift under the Christmas tree. Your child will smile when you spend time with them playing games or just holding them in your arms.

As your child grows up, the smile will come in different forms. It may be the result of a corny "dad joke" or cheering them on from the sidelines. You may see it from the stage when their eyes connect with yours after searching through a sea of parents in the audience. You will also strive for that tired smile that reveals itself after the tears stop flowing and they know that despite whatever burdens their heart, you are there with them.

To see that smile, you will find a strength that you never knew you possessed. By God's grace, you will do many things for your child, but who you are and how you love them, not in possessions but in time, will secure that many years from now, when they remember their old man, they will find themselves smiling as they get lost in their precious memories.

Prayer

God of love, I am grateful for this invitation to be this child's father. Protect them and their mom; keep them safe, strong, and healthy. Give me the strength and grace to support them, not just during this pregnancy, but for as long as I am alive.

✏️ Love Note

Use the space below to write a short note to your child. (Recommendation: Recall a time when you found yourself smiling during this pregnancy. Share what happened and what you thought.)

_____
_____
_____
_____
_____
_____
_____
_____
_____
_____
_____
_____
_____
_____
_____
_____
_____
_____
_____
_____

Thirty Weeks Pregnant: This Little Light

Scripture

"You are the light of the world" (Matt 5:14).

In the Mother's Womb

With ten weeks to go, your baby now weighs three pounds. Their eyes are becoming stronger and they can tell the difference between light and dark. Babies can even follow a light source with their eyes.

In the Father's Heart

For almost two decades, I ministered to college students as a campus minister. I would often say to them, in awe of their maturity, kindness, and faith, how I hoped my kids would be like them when older.

For ten of those years, I directed a faith-based scholarship program called the Catholic Scholars, which invited students to see themselves as the "light of the world." You must also model this for your children, inviting them to use their gifts and talents to be light amid so much darkness. You will accomplish this by inviting them into an intimate relationship with Jesus and into a community of faith and friendship that will support them on the journey.

As their first teacher, it is your actions that will speak louder than your words—no easy task. You will work daily to shine your own light for your children and others to receive and follow.

When my oldest, Shea, received her first holy communion, it was apparent how seriously she took this occasion as she practiced diligently and said her prayers during Mass. She understood how special this sacrament was to her relationship with Jesus. I credit not only us as her parents but also her faith community at school, which formed her. Even at seven years old, she knew how critical it was to be in union with God, and as a result, she shines God's divine light for others.

Prayer

God of light, from the smallest of sparks, a child was conceived and is now growing in the darkness of their mother's womb. They will soon be in this world and bring joy to so many who welcome them with open hearts and arms. As they grow older, help them remember that they shine your light. Help me remember this, too, and model it for my family, as they will walk in my ways.

Love Note

Use the space below to write a short note to your child. (Recommendation: Share a story about a person who shined brightly in your life. How did they make you feel? What did they say or do?)

Thirty-one Weeks Pregnant: Strength

Scripture

"From the end of the earth I call you, when my heart is faint" (Ps 61:2).

In the Mother's Womb

Your baby is the size of a bunch of asparagus. Mom may feel more tired and even struggle to breathe, as the baby is over 15.5 inches long, pushing the uterus, and possibly crowding mom's lungs. Mom may also start to feel that simple tasks are more difficult and sleeping is more challenging. Doctor visits will increase in frequency.

In the Father's Heart

Seeing mom struggle is difficult. Your best efforts, although appreciated, may not make life easier for mom as baby gets bigger and stronger.

You may also face internal challenges as you get closer to delivery. Fears related to finances, space, and work-life balance may arise. At the same time, you may be growing in self-confidence and in your own abilities. These feelings may all strengthen in intensity.

As you remain strong, brave, and present for mom, identify your support network, friends, and family, who can listen, offer you words of wisdom, and share in some laughs. Find time to pray, reset, and not lose focus on the miracle developing in front of you. You are not called to be perfect. Simply be, and allow God to strengthen and guide you.

Prayer

Blessed Mother, I call upon your intercession again for the mother of our child. You know the pains of pregnancy, the fears and realities that make this time so challenging. As you leaned on St. Joseph, and trusted in God, guide my partner in your ways. And guide me to love her, to be her silent and steady rock, as your earthly support was for you.

✎ Love Note

Use the space below to write a short note to your child. (Recommendation: Share with your child the names of those you turn to when life may become difficult. Who are your coaches and teammates? Thank God for them and share some anecdotes.)

Thirty-Two Weeks Pregnant: What's In a Name

Scripture

> "A good name is better than precious ointment…" (Eccl 7:1).

In the Mother's Womb

About the size of a bunch of celery, your baby is now over 16 inches long. They are gaining more fat and have a full head of hair, just as they will when they are born two months from now.

In the Father's Heart

When we had our first child, I wanted to name her Shea, after the long-time home of the New York Mets, Shea Stadium. I also had a mentor and friend who passed away unexpectedly a few years prior whose maiden name was Shea. Shea is also short for Sheamus, an Irish translation for James, the name of both my dad and myself.

My wife said if she comes out with orange hair, we could, perhaps reluctantly, name her Shea. I almost brought a small, orange-colored wig to the maternity ward. When Shea was born, her hair cooperated, and after a few days of conversation, mom finally agreed—our daughter's name was Shea.

When our second child was about to be born, Shea started calling her baby doll, "baby Lily." Suzie and I turned to each other, and we smiled, both liking this name. We waited to meet her, and Lily felt perfect. She also reminded me of a special aunt named Lillian, who had that special knack to make you feel like the most important person in the world. They both have middle names that honor other loved ones and the Blessed Mother.

What name(s) did you choose for your child? Will it honor a loved one or saint, capture the symbolism of desired traits, or will it just fit your baby when your eyes meet theirs?

Pray with mom and be open to where the Holy Spirit moves you in your discernment and creativity.

Prayer

Holy Spirit, Great Counselor, guide us as we prepare names for our baby. We seek to honor the love that brought this child into being through the generations and our faith, serving as a constant reminder to our child that they are your beloved, always.

✎ Love Note

Use the space below to write a short note to your child. (Recommendation: Share with your child why you chose their name. Discuss what the conversation was like with mom and how you came to this decision).

Thirty-three Weeks Pregnant: Growing Stronger

Scripture

> "So the Lord God caused a deep sleep to fall upon the man, and he slept; then he took one of his ribs and closed up its place with flesh" (Gen 2:21).

In the Mother's Womb

Your baby is now the size of a pineapple, and their brain and nervous system are fully developed. Your baby's bones are also beginning to harden.

In the Father's Heart

The creation stories in the book of Genesis reveal several truths. Two of these truths are that we are made in God's image and likeness and that we are not meant to be alone. God created a partner for you, not just for companionship, but to nurture life in this world. Through traditional fatherhood and other vocations like teaching, coaching, and mentoring, you fulfill this call.

As your child's bones grow stronger and as they prepare for their life on earth, this is a moment to recognize again what God is doing. Your child, made in God's image and likeness, will soon set forth on their life journey. You will accompany them, revealing God's love in words and action.

Never lose sight of your role in the miraculous. As St. Mother Teresa is credited with saying, "I'm a little pencil in the hand of a writing God, who is sending a love letter to the world."[19] As a father, you are starting to write your greatest love letter.

Prayer

My Creator, I write this new love letter as your instrument. I am humbled and excited to be in service through you and for you. This shift in perspective allows me to see this role as greater than my domestic family and as just a small yet critical piece in a much larger tapestry. May I be reminded of this often, so that I am not consumed by my own challenges and joys, but also aware and committed to the larger story being written by you.

✎ Love Note

Use the space below to write a short note to your child. (Recommendation: Take this time to share how you are feeling. What are your hopes and dreams as you approach these final months?)

_____
_____
_____
_____
_____
_____
_____
_____
_____
_____
_____
_____
_____
_____
_____
_____
_____
_____
_____

Thirty-four Weeks Pregnant: Finishing Touches

Scripture

> "Do not fear, for I am with you, do not be afraid, for I am your God; I will strengthen you, I will help you, I will uphold you with my victorious right hand" (Isa 41:10).

In the Mother's Womb

Go to the grocery store today and pick up a standard five-pound bag of flour. That is the size of your baby. While doctors prefer the baby to not be born until week thirty-eight, their chance of survival is very high at this point in the pregnancy.

In the Father's Heart

When my oldest was a little over a month away from being born, as your child is now, her bedroom was all set. The crib was assembled, the walls painted, and new drawers were starting to be filled with onesies and diapers. The room was ready even though I wasn't.

Soon, the room, like life, would become messy, but the most perfect little baby would rest in that crib. There is something quite special about preparing the way for your child. As you experience this time, it may feel long and drawn out. In hindsight, it goes so very quickly. You do not get these days again. Pay attention to the preparation that is occurring, not just in this transformed room, but in your heart.

Just imagine how God felt about us as he prepared others to love us into being, and how God accompanied our parents as they prepared a space for us to rest and to grow. Imagine what God must have felt as he designed us, in his image and likeness, to live and to love. Imagine what he feels now as you fulfill your destiny.

You, dad, are coming to fruition. The time of preparation is almost complete.

Prayer

God of Peace, as I strive for perfection, I am often humbled knowing that this is not possible. I seek only to satisfy you by being and doing my best for my family. May I be reminded of this as I prepare for the birth of my and your child.

✎ Love Note

Use the space below to write a short note to your child. (Recommendation: Share stories of preparing space for your child. Describe what you did to transform this space and how you felt as you put the finishing touches on their new place of rest.)

_____
_____
_____
_____
_____
_____
_____
_____
_____
_____
_____
_____
_____
_____
_____
_____
_____

Thirty-five Weeks Pregnant: Love's Destiny

Scripture

> "Every generous act of giving, with every perfect gift, is from above, coming down from the Father of lights, with whom there is no variation or shadow due to change" (Jas 1:17).

In the Mother's Womb

Mom might be ready for baby to come out by now, as the uterus now reaches under her rib cage. She may be feeling heartburn, headaches, and overall tiredness. Since baby is so big, there is less room for baby to move around—but they are still kicking and stretching.

In the Father's Heart

Thomas Merton wrote, "Love is our true destiny. We do not find the meaning of life by ourselves alone—we find it with another."[20] You are reminded of this love as a miracle is unfolding before you. As baby grows and mom transforms into a vessel of love, you can look into mom's eyes and see that what Merton wrote rings true. When your baby is born, you will understand this even more.

When my second, Lily, was born, she wouldn't sleep unless we were holding her. Because it was during the first months of the COVID-19 pandemic, we obliged. I took the 8 p.m. to 3 a.m. shift, where we watched sitcom reruns and dozed off a bit. I also wrote much of my second book, *Batter Up: Answering the Call of Faith & Fatherhood*, with Lily's head on my shoulder. Due to the preciousness of that time,

I stopped often to truly see the gift sleeping in my arms. Love was revealed in each tiny breath, and although I was exhausted, she gave me a strength I never knew existed.

Soon, you will hold your child, and Merton's words will be fulfilled. Until then, be present to love's destiny that God is preparing for you and revealing to you in mom, your loved ones, and the many who accompany your growing family.

Prayer

God of love, you bless me with your love and reveal it through your creation. As I pause and look around and see your love revealed in my friends and family, my heart is filled with gratitude. Thank you.

📝 Love Note

Use the space below to write a short note to your child. (Recommendation: Write about someone who revealed God's love to you, especially when you were most vulnerable.)

Thirty-six Weeks Pregnant: These Things

Scripture

> "Finally, beloved, whatever is true, whatever is honorable, whatever is just, whatever is pure, whatever is pleasing, whatever is commendable, if there is any excellence and if there is anything worthy of praise, think about these things" (Phil 4:8).

In the Mother's Womb

You made it to the ninth month, and your baby now weighs about 6 to 7 pounds. Doctor visits are now weekly, and the anticipation is building. You may even want to get that "to-go bag" ready and install the car seat.

In the Father's Heart

You will likely do many wonderful things during your time here on earth. You probably have already made the world better by the sharing of your life and love. Consider all the ways you revealed God's love—all the people touched by your kindness, your generosity of gifts, your friendship and faith. Now, God calls you into a new chapter, while continuing to nourish those previous relationships. As this time of preparation nears its conclusion, you may try to anticipate the birth of your child and what it will be and feel like. Yet, whatever you imagine, it will not come close to what you will experience in just a few weeks.

You are likely feeling a variety of emotions, ranging from fear to peaceful joy. Whatever you are feeling in this moment, remember and live the words above that St. Paul wrote to the Christian community in Philippi. Keep your heart and mind focused here and trust that all will be well.

Prayer

Lord, I rejoice in your ways. I am blessed by your gentle hand that guides me to this very moment. I know I am experiencing the miraculous, and I pray that my head and heart will focus more on this and you, instead of the noise and distractions that keep me from being present to this very moment.

📝 Love Note

Use the space below to write a short note to your child. (Recommendation: Pray with the words of St. Paul and try to capture what you are feeling as your baby is almost here.)

Thirty-seven Weeks Pregnant: This Season

Scripture

> "For everything there is a season, and a time for every matter under heaven" (Eccl 3:1).

In the Mother's Womb

Your baby is getting ready to make their grand entrance as they are practicing inhaling, exhaling, blinking, and sucking. They are the size of a head of romaine lettuce, gaining at least half an ounce each day.

In the Father's Heart

I have wasted so much energy and time trying to control what could/would/should happen in my life. When a child is coming, and the stakes are so high, it is only natural that we, as dads, would want to control the future to protect those we love.

Parenthood quickly invites and, probably more realistically, forces you to the spiritual practice of surrender. This doesn't mean you shouldn't prepare or not be responsible, but there is so much out of your control.

Life can be more joyful and peaceful if you fully surrender to God. This involves an incredible amount of trust. Be patient with yourself, as it is a life-long process. Trusting and letting go of the need to control also becomes a life lesson that you will teach your children.

There have been many reflective nights when I turned to the famous Beatles hit, "Let it Be," before closing my eyes.

This song echoes true through the decades as it speaks a truth and an underlying trust that all will be well.

St. Elizabeth Ann Seton teaches us, "Faith lifts the soul, hope supports it, experience says it must and love says let it be."[21]

Prayer

God of peace, as the pressure mounts and the weeks soon become days, I seek to center my mind and heart on you and trust in your divine plan. Help me remember that you are with me, always.

✏️ Love Note

Use the space below to write a short note to your child. (Recommendation: Try to capture what you are feeling in words.)

Thirty-eight Weeks Pregnant: Food for the Soul

Scripture

> "And Jesus said to them, 'I am the bread of life. Whoever comes to me will never be hungry, and whoever believes in me will never be thirsty'" (John 6:35).

In the Mother's Womb

Labor usually starts between weeks thirty-eight and forty. Your baby weighs over 6 pounds, and the hair that covered your child for warmth is falling off. Their vocal cords are ready to communicate.

In the Father's Heart

While mom is likely limited in her physical abilities, this is a time to get busy in the kitchen. The first few weeks of your newborn's life will be hectic, so preparing some meals in advance will save time and money. I can recall freezing trays of food that were answers to prayers when we were sleep-deprived, hungry, and slightly irritable.

As you prepare these meals, continue to find time to prepare your heart and soul. How are you feeding your spirit for what is to come? Secure time for spiritual reading and prayer (in addition to these pages).

You are being called into service at all moments, and the delivery will likely be frightening for all involved. This is the time to prepare spiritually for what will be a holistic challenge. Prioritize your relationship with God so, just as

St. Peter was the rock for the Church, you can be the rock for your own holy family.

You are also being called into wisdom to lead your family, by inspiration, faith, and trust. Pope Francis reminds us that, "Nothing could better express the pride and emotion a father feels when he understands that he has handed down to his child what really matters in life, that is, a wise heart."[22]

Prayer

God of nourishment and fulfillment, I turn to you to fill my cup as I fill that of my wife and growing child. With each act of love, I know I am not only serving them, but I am serving you. Grant me the strength and grace to be your instrument of love.

✏️ Love Note

Use the space below to write a short note to your child. (Recommendation: Describe your prayers with God. What did you offer up and how did you feel? Share these thoughts so your child, many years from now, might consider doing the same.)

_____

_____

_____

_____

_____

_____

_____

_____

_____

_____

_____

_____

_____

_____

_____

_____

_____

_____

Thirty-nine Weeks Pregnant: Almost Time

Scripture

> "For this child I prayed: and the Lord has granted me the petition that I made to him" (1 Sam 1:27).

In the Mother's Womb

Your baby is the size of a watermelon (just imagine what mom is feeling). Your baby is now considered full-term, and they probably reached their birth weight. It is time to watch for signs of labor.

In the Father's Heart

Remember when you used to go to sleep at night with carefree thoughts? Those days are no more, as now you are likely on edge, waiting for mom to say, "It is time."

All our paths to fatherhood vary. Some of us have waited a very long time for this moment, while for others, it may be quite unexpected, and maybe at first, even unwanted. You may also be somewhere in between. I trust that there was a point, even if it was hidden in the silence of your heart, that this call to fatherhood was met with purpose and acceptance.

As a young man, I knew I would be a dad one day, even if my dating life was inactive. I just sensed that I was meant to be a father, and this has been affirmed daily since my daughters were born.

During this pregnancy, your emotions took you on a roller coaster of highs and lows, self-reflections that journeyed from fear to joy, insecurities to confidence. You are ready.

It is almost time for God to call you into this next chapter of your life, and the first chapter for your child. You have been a father for thirty-nine weeks, caring for this forming child and their mom. Soon, you will reap the fruits of this (and mom's) labor, to hold the answer to your prayers.

Prayer

Lord God, I am ready. Beyond my fears and concerns, I was prepared by you for this moment. Protect my partner and my child, and all others who wait in joyful anticipation.

✏️ Love Note

Use the space below to write a short note to your child. (Recommendation: Spend time recalling the last thirty-nine weeks. Highlight some of the moments that resurface and not only describe them but reflect on how they make you feel now.)

Forty Weeks Pregnant: Love

Scripture

"Hear my prayer, O God; give ear to the words of my mouth" (Ps 54:2).

In the Mother's Womb

About the size of a small pumpkin, your baby is ready to be born. Your baby's had time to fully develop and is ready to meet their mom and dad. Mom is exhausted, likely dealing with aches and pains, and the simplest of tasks are daunting.

In the Father's Heart

When my first child was about to be born, my wife spent four throbbing days in labor. Short walks and warm baths filled our days. When our second child was born, we had a scheduled caesarian section, so there was no ambiguity of date or time, other than the fact that it was in the heart of the COVID-19 pandemic, and fears of health and safety were at an all-time high. I remember not wanting to leave my wife's side both times. I felt helpless as there was so little I could do for her other than get her the medical care that she and our baby needed.

This feeling of helplessness forced me to pray, as it was the only task I could do to help. I was left to trust and accept that "God's will be done," praying it would lead to a happy ending. I wasn't ready to lose my wife, and how desperately I wanted to hold those babies in my arms.

These words attributed to St. Mother Teresa of Calcutta rang true then as they do now, "Love to be real, it must cost—it must hurt—it must empty us of self." From a distance, I struggle to learn this lesson—to empty myself and to trust fully in God's will. Not just in moments of crisis, but in our daily lives—to trust in God and to love to the point of full acceptance and trust.

Prayer

Father of beauty, I surrender to you. Any illusion that I am in control is gone, and I turn to you for your protection and intervention to bring my baby and mom through the delivery so we can be a holy family in service to you and others.

✎ Love Note

Use the space below to write a short note to your child. (Recommendation: Write your prayer to God for mom and baby.)

Your Baby is Born

Scripture

> "Yet it was you who took me from the womb; you kept me safe on my mother's breast. On you I was cast from my birth, and since my mother bore me you have been my God" (Ps 22:9–10).

In the Mother's Heart

For the past nine-plus months, mom's blessed womb protected your baby as they grew from a divine spark into the baby you now hold. Mom's heart, like yours, is also transformed as she finally sees what her body has felt. Don't miss the miracle of mom's presence, as her beauty has never shined like this before.

In the Father's Heart

There are no words to describe what you are feeling. Simply marvel at this miracle. When I talk with first-time dads, I love to ask what it was like when they saw their baby for the first time. Even the most articulate of men struggle to describe what happens when they meet their child.

When I met my oldest, I marveled at her beauty and desired to hold her, which was delayed due to a short stay in the NICU. When my youngest was born, I held her only briefly, as urgently and gently, I placed her in her car seat as we were in the heart of the pandemic. My only thought was, "She is so tiny."

They are so fragile, and that slow drive home from the hospital each time reflected this. I wonder if we could approach all life with that same appreciation, caution, and sensitivity.

Take photos and videos to capture this moment. Remember to also be present, absorbing this beauty with every power of your being. Congratulations my friend, your life will never be the same.

Prayer

This is adapted from a prayer of St. Augustine: Father, I am seeking: I am hesitant and uncertain, but will you, O God, watch over each step of mine and guide me as I serve as this baby's father? Watch, too, over each step of my child, and guide them in your ways.

✎ Love Note

Use the space below to write a short note to your child. (Recommendation: Write your prayer to God for your child on these first days of their life.)

Loss

You may have started this book and engaged in its reflective practice, filled with hope and excitement. Then, everything may have changed at some point during the pregnancy or after the birth of your child.

Right from the very beginning of the writing process, I was fearful of writing this book for those who would suffer the devastating loss of a child. I initially had this fear just a few weeks before my wife and I suffered a miscarriage during her second pregnancy. I looked far and wide for resources to make sense of it all, but nothing helped.

I believe there is space for our Church and society to support dads who are supporting mom while also grieving and healing. Where can men turn when their heart is broken?

According to the National Library of Medicine, an estimated twenty-three million miscarriages occur every year worldwide, translating to forty-four pregnancy losses each minute and 15 percent of all pregnancies.[23] According to the organization, Save the Children, "the first 28 days of a child's life—the neonatal, or newborn, period—carries the highest risk of death. It is also the most dangerous period for the newborn's mother. Each year, 2.4 million newborns die, 1.9 million babies are stillborn, and 295,000 women die globally during pregnancy or childbirth. More than 800,000 newborns die on the first day of life, making the day of birth the most dangerous day for babies in nearly every country."[24]

After the doctor told us the horrific news, we sat in his office crying. He referenced the statistics, but this did not help us other than to give us a sense of solidarity with so many others who were experiencing pain. I share this knowing that, if you are reading these words and experiencing this heartbreak, it brings you little consolation. I share it only to exemplify that you are not alone, and that there are millions of dads who have been crushed by a devastating ending to what was supposed to be one of life's most joyful chapters. If this is your story, I humbly offer some thoughts on how you might move forward when ready. This book serves a different purpose, and I pray if you are blessed with another pregnancy, that these pages will accompany you all the way to the day you can hold your child. For now, before you close this book and tuck it away in some box or drawer, a few thoughts.

1. *Mark the Loss*: Find a way to create a ritual to acknowledge this enormous loss. Some will have a funeral service and/or Mass. Others will name the child. This is a decision you and mom will make together. A spiritual mentor advised me, knowing my love for creating, to paint on a blank canvas in honor of my lost child. I did this about twelve weeks after the miscarriage, and it produced something I could hold. The painting now sits in my office, no longer a reminder of loss (although some of the sting remains), but it brings me hope for the next life, when we will be reunited.

2. *Find Community*: Faith communities can do a better job in creating these spaces for men, as they do for other areas of bereavement. Unless this is formed already, find ways to be with other dads who are struggling or have struggled with this loss. These heart-to-heart conversations may occur over a beer, with a game on in the background, so be open to the possibility, listen with

your heart, and resist the temptation to provide or search for answers. Over time, you will be the one with the experience to offer a listening ear and to model that life, although never the same, does continue.

3. *Mourn with Mom*: You will want to be strong for her. Her physical, emotional, spiritual, and psychological challenges are real and heightened. You may not be able to unload your heart, but sharing that you accompany her in carrying this cross, will only strengthen your union. You may even find that sharing your pain will bring you closer and that this experience may eventually even strengthen your relationship.

4. *Turn to God*: In moments of crisis, we are literally sent to our knees. Allow this to be a time of reunion, where you can surrender it all to your Creator. Find time in silence to unload what is in your heart and mind. Listen and be open to God's amazing grace that will support each step that you take. Seek counsel from spiritual leaders who can listen objectively, wipe your tears away, and remind you of God's compassion.

This is adapted from a St. Catherine of Siena quotation: "To the brave man, good and bad experiences* are like his right and left hand. He uses both." I am not sure I can describe the loss of a child as bad luck, nor do I wish to cast blame on God or anyone else. Rather, this quotation offers an invitation. How can this sorrow eventually shift into something fruitful?

---

* I changed the word *luck* for *experiences* as it seemed more appropriate for the nature of this chapter.

Will you become a support for a future dad when they walk this familiar path? Will you see the next pregnancy (God-willing) with wider and clearer eyes? Will you allow this cross to deepen the depth of your own heart and will you meet Christ there?

May your child be entrusted into God's care, and I pray they will meet you when you transition to your eternal home. May you and mom find God's love and comfort in the days, weeks, and months ahead, and may you find the healing that you seek.

I am fortunate to host a podcast with Focolare Media titled, *Home Run Fathers*, where we interview men with a variety of life experiences, including some version of fatherhood. Guests have included fathers, stepfathers, grandfathers, a priest, a minister, and leaders in parishes, civic communities, and athletics. One interview brought me to tears. It was with Mike Zwartjes, a member of the Focolare Community. Mike, with his wife, Jeannette, lost their five-year-old son, John, in 1991, to an illness. Twenty-three years later, Mike, now a grandfather to one of his two surviving son's children, shared joyfully about John, and the many lessons he learned over his years of fatherhood.

In 2016, New City Press published a deeply moving book capturing John's short yet impactful life titled *John of the Smiles*. Talented author Geraldine Guadagno masterfully tells the story with Mike and Jeanette. At the conclusion of the Introduction to *John of the Smiles*, Guadagno includes a selection from the writings of John Henry Cardinal Newman, which, in Guadagno's words, "provides a context for John's life."[25] Newman's words not only capture John's short journey, they also call us forward when we are standing in the shadow of death and when life doesn't turn out as expected:

God has created me to do Him some definite service; He has committed some work to me which He has not committed to another. I have my mission—I never may know it in this life, but I shall be told it in the next. Somehow I am necessary for His purposes, as necessary in my place as an Archangel in his—if, indeed, I fail, He can raise another, as He could make the stones children of Abraham. Yet I have a part in this great work; I am a link in a chain, a bond of connexion between persons. He has not created me for naught. I shall do good, I shall do His work; I shall be an angel of peace, a preacher of truth in my own place, while not intending it, if I do but keep His commandments and serve Him in my calling.

Therefore, I will trust Him. Whatever, wherever I am, I can never be thrown away. If I am in sickness, my sickness may serve Him; in perplexity, my perplexity may serve Him; if I am in sorrow, my sorrow may serve Him. My sickness, or perplexity, or sorrow may be necessary causes of some great end, which is quite beyond us. He does nothing in vain; He may prolong my life, He may shorten it; He knows what He is about. He may take away my friends, He may throw me among strangers, He may make me feel desolate, make my spirits sink, hide the future from me—still He knows what He is about.

O Emmanuel ... I give myself to Thee. I trust Thee wholly. Thou art wiser than I—more loving to me than I myself. Deign to fulfil Thy high purposes in me whatever they be—work in and through me. I am born to serve Thee, to be Thine, to be

> Thy instrument ... I ask not to see—I ask not to know—I ask simply to be used.[26]

It is truly remarkable to think of a sick child who captured these wise words. I wonder, in our own challenges when our raw wounds are at their deepest and most painful, if we can exemplify this trust in God. It is perhaps not possible, as one must grieve and heal. Perhaps these words are a north star to guide us when we are at our darkest. May these words be your prayer, urging you to not only find God in the heartbreak but also to trust him there.

Our Moms

Although we mentioned mom throughout these pages, this chapter is solely dedicated to her. We begin by looking at our own mothers, then the mothers of our children, plus all the mother figures in our life, both spiritually and practically. This book is focused on you—the dad. Yet, this is not a path you take alone. There is a mom involved, serving as more than a vessel for your child but a child of God undergoing her own transformation.

As noted in the opening chapter, I am sensitive to the various realities that face you, the reader. The mother of your child may very well be your wife, your life partner, and your best friend. Perhaps she once filled that role, but now, after some bumps and bruises, she is now the mother of your child, and that alone. She may even be the mother of your adopted child, a stranger until your life's paths crossed.

Whatever the situation, the baby in your arms was formed by God, in the womb of their mother. No matter where she stands in your list of admired figures, she will always be that—and for that, we must honor her, love her, and greet her with empathy, kindness, and support.

Your Mom

As we venture down this road of admiration, let's start with your own beginnings when you were formed in your mother's womb. You do not remember this in your intellectual mind, but in the depths of your being, you will recall where it all started. It was here where you were first nurtured and supported. The sound you first heard was your mom's heartbeat that worked tirelessly above your developing body, not just for herself, but for you. She carried you, cautious of all she ate, drank, and inhaled. She sacrificed her body, her mind, her health, and maybe even some other dreams, so you could be born.

This isn't meant to form guilt but rather an appreciation for one human creating another. With courage and strength, she carried you into labor, when you were either pulled out or cut from her body. As a miracle—there is no other explanation—you entered the world, and it was your mom who held you close to her chest, where that familiar heart pounded into your now-developed ears.

Soon, you grew in size and in wisdom. Your mom, and dad, along with a small village, held, fed, and cleaned you, forming you into the person you would become. Other voices would smooth your edges, and you found your way. Your biological mom may have been the best in the world, or she may have had more faults than you prefer to recall. You may also never have known her at all.

No matter what she did, she gave you life. And if you are among the many who hoped for a mom who hugged more than yelled, cared more than cursed, and loved more than anyone else could, then this call for admiration and honor is going to be a challenge for you on your spiritual and psychological journey. You may have to set boundaries, see your mom with her wounds, and forgive her. This call for mercy to forgive her may occur with her not present in your life. Forgiveness becomes a gift for yourself. It will be the most difficult decision you will make in this life, but it will make you a freer person, more capable of love than you can even imagine. Your children deserve this from you, even if you didn't receive it from your parent. You will also learn how to love and not make the same mistakes. You will make different decisions and parent in other ways to avoid becoming what you once feared and disliked. You can be the dad to your children that she was unable to be as your mother.

On the other hand, your mom may have been present, loving, and kind. Never perfect, but you always knew she cared and loved you. I am blessed to be in that company, and I owe much of my spiritual path as a writer and dad to her example. If this is your experience, recall memories when your mom brought you comfort like no one else could. In her honor, replicate it for your child.

On one occasion, I recall being around nine years old and battling a bad virus. I slept all weekend so I could watch the then-World Wrestling Federation's (WWF) Summer Slam that Sunday night, a professional wrestling pay-per-view. While I was sick, my mom made her famous chicken soup, or pastina, an Italian dish of tiny pasta, eggs, salt, and water. What stands out from this illness, as if it was yesterday, is that I can still taste that dinner before the main event: homemade grilled cheese sandwich, cold pickles, and sweet iced tea.

Today, when my kids are recovering from a cold, I make soup, just like my mom. But when the fever breaks and the kids start to turn the corner, I feel the need to make them a grilled cheese sandwich. It brought so much comfort that it left a mark decades ago.

It is important to create these traditions that connect generations, even if its impact does not match your experience. There is a silent and hidden thread that runs through us all, and whenever we can tap into those moments, we reconnect with a love that is deeper than our imagination can comprehend.

Mother Figures

You surely had many other women in your life who stepped into a mothering role: grandmothers, Godmothers, aunts, older sisters and cousins, teachers, religious leaders and sisters, coaches, and maybe even now, your mother-in-law, to name a few. These women love you in a different way than your mom. They offered consolation, support, and small cracks in the breaking of rules that led to a special dessert or a later bedtime. They provided comfort and care in those moments of your life when your need met their purpose. They healed your wounds, formed your spirit, and inspired your own path to fatherhood.

In the final editing of the first draft of this book, I said goodbye to my grandmother, Margaret "Peggy" Walters. She lived to the age of ninety-three but suffered for the last eight years of her life battling dementia and a slow physical decline. When my wife and I visited her to say goodbye in her final days, I was blessed to be met by her beautiful smile and sparkling eyes. Although she was frail and her breathing labored, her spirit was still felt in that encounter.

At one point during our visit, I was rubbing her straight white hair. Two years prior, as she started to prepare for this transition, her hair turned perfectly white. For the forty-plus years that I knew her, she always dyed her hair a light brown or blonde, and it was often curly and short. As my hand ran through her hair in this final encounter, it was nothing short of angelic. She was comforted by the touch, closing her eyes and exhaling. Birds outside began to chirp, and she turned her head slightly to acknowledge their presence.

Later that night, I rested with Lily who was just about to turn four. She had a nightmare and couldn't fall asleep. Just hours before, I was rubbing my grandmother's hair. Now, I was rubbing my Lily's. I couldn't ignore the symmetry, as one was just ending her journey and the other just beginning it. This was middle age, I thought, caught between a great-grandmother and her great-granddaughter. In the silence, I was comforting both as they found rest and peace.

We accompany one another in this life, a short window of time when we are fortunate and blessed to share. The child will one day care for their parents or, in this case, the grandson, caring for his grandmother and his own daughter. They both were agitated, vulnerable, and scared. A warm embrace, not by me but by God through me, brought some peace to my loved ones.

This is who we are called to be—an instrument of God. Many others have and will accompany us through the ordinary and extraordinary. We, in return, accompany others.

The child you now love and nourish will one day, God-willing, accompany you as you prepare to return home. If you are as fortunate as my grandmother, it will be your grandchildren or even great-grandchildren who will love you until you return to the source of all our love.

As I watch my daughters grow, I see the many mother figures who complement their own mom. When we pray at night, we name them, asking God for their continued blessings upon them, and we share our gratitude. As these little girls recall the names of today's saints, they smile and know a small village supports them in the pursuit of all their dreams.

Honor these women by telling them who they are to you. As I wrote my first book, I thanked, in the opening pages, my sophomore-year math teacher, Mrs. Lorraine Smith. She spent many early mornings teaching me the previous day's algebra lessons. Mrs. Smith had the patience of a saint, and that B at the end of the year would never have happened if it wasn't for her sacrifice. She had to get up early, get her own kids off to school, and make her way to her classroom forty minutes early just to help one artsy and somewhat awkward student with a love for the Mets and a tumultuous relationship with Algebra 2.

Fast forward to 2021, and I am at a book signing in Cooperstown, New York, during Hall of Fame weekend. It was extra special, as Brooklyn Dodgers and Mets legend Gil Hodges, was being inducted. His son, Gil Hodges, Jr., was gracious enough to endorse my second book only months before.

At the signing, who shows up but Mrs. Smith. She was visiting family about an hour away and took time on this busy and hot Saturday morning to visit her former student. As those legendary teachers often do, Mrs. Smith taught me another lesson that day. The importance of showing up. It meant more to me than she could ever realize. As you examine your relationships, when the opportunity presents itself to show up, always do!

Religious Sisters

I am also fortunate to be formed by many wonderful women who are family, friends, teachers, and employers. I serve as the NGO (non-governmental organization) Representative for the Sisters of Charity Federation. I am blessed to represent nearly two thousand religious sisters in twenty-five countries.

Since joining their mission of charity in late 2022, I find myself surrounded by heroic women who dedicate their lives to service, faith, and love. I always appreciated religious sisters. Many served as my educators throughout several decades of Catholic education. They live the Gospel with authenticity and work tirelessly for others.

As the sisters invite me into their world and share their charism of charity, I see another transformation occurring. As Blessed Frederic Ozanam learned to serve those in poverty in nineteenth-century France, I am learning how to serve and advocate for justice at the United Nations from the Sisters of Charity and the many other religious congregations who advocate for human rights.

While these religious sisters do not have biological children, they have mothered countless children in hospitals, schools, orphanages, shelters, churches, and other missions and ministries. There are generations who felt the touch of God's unconditional love through these wisdom figures and good and faithful servants. I stand in awe of them and pray my work and ministry will continue what they started so many years ago.

As you now hold your child, memories of your past will flow like the wine at that famous wedding in Cana. In your baby, you will see facial gestures and similarities that will remind you of past generations. When you open your mouth, you will hear voices of the past echo. As you tend to your child, you will recall those who nurtured you and lifted you up.

When these memories sneak in like the first morning light, say a silent prayer of gratitude. If these loved ones are still with you, send a note, or a text filled with your thanks. If they have already returned home to God, send a silent prayer trusting it is received.

Look to your mom and maternal figures and cherish what they poured into your soul. Look to your baby's mom, too. They bring us closer to our Creator, reminding us of who we are—God's beloved.

Hail Mary

In this chapter, we explored your mother figures but we haven't turned our attention to our beloved mother in heaven, Mary, Jesus' mom, who was brave enough to say yes, to bring the Son of God into being, and to watch him do the miraculous.

I have had a special devotion to Mary ever since I was a child. When I was seven, my mom was very sick. I saw her spend each night in prayer as she read what felt like hundreds of prayer cards and novenas. The rosary beads were never far behind. I started to pray like she taught me, especially during her surgery and hospital visits. I feared that if I didn't pray, something worse would happen to her. When I fell asleep in prayer, I woke up feeling guilty. Only later did I learn that there was no better way to end a day.

As my spirituality matured, my prayer changed. My formation was most influenced by two Marian apparitions—the healing waters of Lourdes, France, and the Miraculous Medal in Paris, France.

I was blessed to bring students from St. John's University to Lourdes on three separate occasions from 2006–2008, and I returned to visit in 2012. Before going to Lourdes, a friend described it as "heaven on earth." He was right. The last are first and the first are last. Our shared purpose was to bring those seeking physical, spiritual, emotional, or psychological healing to the miraculous water that Mary revealed to St. Bernadette Soubirous in the 1800s.

The Church recognizes seventy miracles from the intervention of God with the intercession of Our Lady of Lourdes. There are many other reports of healing that will never receive the official stamp of the Church, yet they transform lives and communities. During my first visit to the grotto, where this miraculous water still flows, I said a silent prayer asking my heavenly mother to find someone to love as a wife. I always felt called to married life, but I had never met someone that I wanted to spend my life with as a partner. Less than one month after the prayer was said, I met someone who would change my world. She became my wife, best friend, and life partner. Mary works quickly.

My second Marian apparition that transformed my spirit was the Miraculous Medal and St. Catherine Labouré. Mary appeared to St. Catherine on two occasions, and on the last encounter, she instructed medals to be made. Miracles were reported by those who wore the medal, and a strong devotion to Our Lady of the Miraculous Medal developed through the generations.

I have worn a medal around my neck for as long as I can remember. During those difficult moments of life, I find myself grabbing for the medal, remembering that I am not alone. For both St. Bernadette and St. Catherine, their lives did not change because of their heavenly encounters. Rather, both lived simple lives following their experiences. They served as religious sisters, dedicating their lives to those in need.

Following the apparitions, St. Bernadette received an education. She learned how to read and write before serving in an infirmary and later as a sacristan. Unfortunately, as a young child she battled cholera, and faced increased health challenges throughout her short life. She died at the young age of thirty-five on April 16, 1879.

Three years prior, St. Catherine Labouré died on December 31, 1876, at the age of seventy. Unlike St. Bernadette, only St. Catherine's confessor and her mother superior knew that she was the recipient of the medal. She spent her life in prayer also caring for the elderly and infirm.

The temptation in life is to be known, to be popular, and to be successful. Yet, we find in these two faithful servants a different way. They were vessels for Mary to communicate her love. We, too, are called to be vessels. May our children and others come to know the love of Mary, and her Son, through our faithful service.

Mary not only uses us as instruments of her love, but she also calls us into relationship with her. She seeks to let us love her as we love our children. When we carry our crosses, she says to us, I understand. When we are afraid and find the inner strength to say yes, she says, I understand. When we ask Jesus for his intercession, seeking a miracle, Mary says again, I understand.

Let us never forget the love of our heavenly mother. Jesus, from the cross, turned to Mary, who was with John, the youngest disciple, and said, "Behold, your son." He then turned to John, and said, "Behold, your mother." (John 19:26–27) This wasn't a mandate meant for just Mary and John. We are all John: "Behold, your mother." And doesn't it bring us peace to know that Jesus says to Mary, "Behold, your son." We are never alone.

God has blessed us with heavenly and earthly mothers, and countless maternal figures who accompany us on this journey. Now, as we begin this new chapter where we become the parent, may we be reminded of the love we have received, and may we replicate it as we give what we have received.

A Mother is Born

The mother of your child experiences her own transformation. In the days and weeks that follow the birth of your baby, she will experience even more physical, emotional, psychological, and spiritual conversion, as she makes sense of the reality that this baby that formed in her womb is now in her arms. She may continue to physically give to this child as she nurses them, and she will join you in lacking sleep as you respond to every sound and tear.

The call to motherhood is an incredible sacrifice, and while it is one of her greatest vocations, God is likely calling her into other roles to reveal his love. This may require new and different responsibilities for you in creating a loving and effective home.

On any given day, I answer emails, write reflections, advocate for justice, take out the garbage, prepare dinner, clean dishes, and fold laundry. Like a baseball player, some days I am called to swing for the fences, while other days, I am bunting a runner over. Everything is important, especially if it supports my wife's success and pursuit of her dreams. I am her teammate, friend, and partner, seeking with her the same goal—to reveal God's love however and wherever we are called to do so.

Our Dads

In the prior chapter, we explored the many maternal figures in your life. Now, let's turn to the paternal figures, who also made you into the person you are today.

As I did at the start of the last chapter, let's reiterate the sensitivity to the various realities readers may have with their fathers and other male influences. Your most important male figure, for better or for worse, may be your biological father. Or it could be someone else, blood-related or not.

As you look back at your life, account for those men who formed you. Your earthly father, grandfather, uncles, priests, religious leaders and brothers, coaches, teachers, spiritual fathers, among others. They shaped how you love, how you speak, and how you act.

Dr. Wayne Dyer, one of my greatest teachers and a leader in spirituality and self-help, spoke often about his own father, who abandoned him, his brother, and his mother when he was a young child. He said that the greatest lesson he ever learned from his father came after his dad's death. He was spiritually called to forgive him when he tracked down his gravesite after a business trip. It was his forgiveness of his dad that opened his life to peace and love. The irony is that Dyer went to the grave not to forgive his father. Instead, he went there to express his frustration and anger. After he unloaded his burden, it was during his drive away from the cemetery that he felt the spiritual nudge to go back and forgive.

In his forgiveness, he found direction, purpose, and eventual success as a writer and speaker. It all started when he forgave the man who was supposed to love him but instead left him abandoned.

This is such a difficult task—to accept your father with all his imperfections. It takes time, external support and guidance, and prayer. Just imagine if the familiar Prodigal Son parable shifted the narrative, and it was the son who had to forgive the selfish and judgmental father. The call for forgiveness would be the same, but the dynamics change and present different challenges.

Forgiveness is as much a gift to dad as it is to son. It frees you and impacts your relationship with him and, ultimately, your children.

Your Dad

I am blessed with a wonderful father. I never questioned his love for me, and I saw him work tirelessly to provide for me and my family. My dad was a successful and honorable electrician who built a business that was well-respected by his community, employees, and customers. He used his company to help people looking for work, and he used his skills to bring people light, heat, and comfort.

During major heat waves or storms, my dad would go on emergency calls, even at his own discomfort. He treated everyone as if they were his family. Even at our parish, he was the first to offer his services to keep the lights on.

When I was sixteen, I worked with my dad during summer break. That experience made me realize that although we had the same name, that is where it stopped when it came to electrical services. I saw him love his work, yet I felt as if I was in a student exchange program in a different country.

As I look back at that summer, it was clear that this field of work was not my calling. However, watching my father do what he loved, no matter how difficult, inspired me to find my own path of joy and impact. I now see, that he was modeling vocation. It was never about me assuming his place, but about finding my own path.

My dad taught me many more lessons. He allowed me to be me—with all my quirkiness, creativity, and uniqueness. He valued education, especially apparent in his support for me as I struggled to adjust to a new high school, and then eight years later, his tears of joy as my sister and I were the first in our family to graduate from college. Most recently, his care for his mother in her final years as she battled a mental and physical decline, his unconditional love was another lesson on how to love.

Father Figures

I was also blessed with a peaceful army of grandfathers, uncles (some blood-related, some not), Godfathers, mentors, coaches, teachers, and spiritual guides. I learned how to lead, how to communicate, and how to walk with empathy and confidence. Scripture teaches us that iron sharpens iron (Prov 27:17). I am living proof of this spiritual wisdom.

Thankfully, we live in a time where fatherhood has broadened to move beyond financial responsibility. Dads clearly serve other purposes, from coaching to teaching to providing a spiritual home. It is refreshing when we see fathers for all that God calls us to be, and when we can be active in the lives of our children and faith communities.

Fathers are partners with their spouses, and that authentic unity and solidarity is the only way to proceed. When parents are on equal footing, children are taught lessons implicitly about partnership, collaboration, and appreciation for others.

One of my greatest teachers, in addition to my dad, is a Marist brother, Mike Sheerin. I first met him at my home parish, where he lived while doing vocation work for his community. A number of years later, when I was a student at St. John's University, we met again, and he spiritually mentored and guided me during a vulnerable time of transition into and through higher education.

When I started my professional ministry, he was my supervisor, and many years later, I was fortunate again to share in young adult ministry with him. I learned so much from his spirituality and leadership, most especially the importance of empathy, grace, and compassion. I learned how to sit with a young adult and accompany them on their faith journey. I saw him love my children and wife, watching an extended family grow before his eyes.

As a religious brother, no one would call him father. But he was, and is, a spiritual father to countless generations of students. I find myself as a parent and spouse replicating his calm voice and echoing his understanding heart. Brother Mike finds great comfort in being a brother and a companion. I am blessed to be on the receiving end of his vocation. As a lay and married man, I look to him, and so many who dedicated their lives to their faith. As priests, brothers, and deacons, I saw many men who said yes to a life of service that varied by the needs in front of them.

Take a moment to account for those father figures who shepherded you along your life and faith journey. Offer gratitude to God for their gift of self and vocation.

Saints

Finally, we must turn our attention to some of those men who walked before us and are lifted in our faith. I would like to focus on two men, St. Joseph and Blessed Frederic Ozanam.

Not one word in Sacred Scripture is attributed to St. Joseph, yet no man has had a greater role in human history other than Jesus, who was both human and divine. St. Joseph showed mercy to Mary upon her pregnancy revelation. He was open to God's ways, believing in the words of the angel Gabriel, who came to him in a dream. St. Joseph protected Mary and Jesus during their travels and found a safe place for Mary's delivery. St. Joseph taught Jesus how to grow in the Jewish faith, to not only know Scripture but to seek God in all of God's creation.

We do not know of Joseph's final days, but we see the fruit of his labor in the years of ministry of his earthly son. I wonder what it was like when Joseph died. Did Jesus cry as he did when his cousin Lazarus passed? Was he there to see his dad transition home?

I like to believe that Jesus was there with Mary. Mirroring that first Nativity, this time Jesus held his father as Mary shed tears of sorrow. I like to imagine Jesus reading the Psalms, and reminding his dad of the lessons Joseph once taught him as a young child. Perhaps Jesus and Mary sat on chairs and Joseph on a bedframe that he himself had built from the ground up. I wonder if the symbolism struck Jesus and Mary as foreshadowing a similar wood that Jesus would be nailed to at his crucifixion. Even in his death, Joseph taught his holy family to mourn and to trust that this was not the end.

I am also reminded of Blessed Frederic Ozanam. In the Introduction, I share a reflection by this nineteenth-century Parisian figure as he finds the words to describe his own inner transformation during the birth of his first child. Ozanam was a college student when he was challenged by a non-Catholic to match his actions to his words. He spoke so confidently about his faith with his peers, but what did it matter if it didn't impact how he lived, especially in service to those living in poverty and on the margins of society?

Under the mentorship of Blessed Rosalie Rendu, a Daughter of Charity, Ozanam learned how to serve. Ozanam, with friends, created the first Society of St. Vincent de Paul

(SSVP) Conference to unite his fellow students in acts of charity. Today, SSVP is present in 155 countries, has eight hundred thousand members in forty-eight thousand conferences, and 1.5 million members and collaborators. Every day, it helps over thirty million people across the globe.[27]

This all started with Ozanam's courageous yes to live his faith, to be open to mentorship, and to bring people together in collaboration and unity to love those that society often dismissed. Arguably, these words spoken by Ozanam are his most well-known:

> "It is our vocation to set people's hearts ablaze, to do what the Son of God did, who came to light a fire on earth in order to set it ablaze with His love."

Complementing this worthy yet enormous task is perhaps a simpler, less familiar, directive:

> "In my life I want to become better and do a little good.[28]

Ozanam reminds us that we are a work in progress, but we have a serious responsibility, not just to our own children, but to a great number of people and communities in need of our time and action. He teaches us how to humbly work with others, especially those we are trying to serve, by listening and understanding from their lived experience.

Our father figures prepared us to be in service to our children and communities. They are nudging us to be men of faith, humble and empathetic, selfless and committed. Future generations are already watching us, looking to see where we put our energy and attention. What a legacy we can leave, like so many before, to our children and communities. We will call them to greatness, as we answer that call right now.

Conclusion

This final chapter brings your pregnancy experience and this book to a close. I thank you for the opportunity to join you during this monumental time in the life of your family.

As you know, now the fun really begins. You are likely performing heroic tasks on little sleep, all the while smiling ear to ear as your baby grows before your eyes. Continuing, and likely growing, is the pressure and expectations that come with the realities of having a child (and potentially children) who are your responsibility. They depend on you for survival, for development, and for forming a relationship with God. In my before-mentioned book, *Batter Up: Answering the Call of Faith & Fatherhood*, I write about the early years of parenthood, the challenges of being a dad, and the lessons learned along the way. *Batter Up* uses the metaphor of baseball to discuss this reality and to celebrate this calling from God.

As this book ends and your journey of fatherhood continues, I share these final words of wisdom and I pray that you, as dad, with your holy family, will only grow closer to God and to one another.

Pope Francis

The first words of wisdom come from the Holy Father, Pope Francis. Starting December 8, 2020, Pope Francis dedicated the following year to St. Joseph. As a result, we have a treasure chest of writings and statements by the Holy Father, some of which have already been provided in this book. Here is one more for your discernment and transformation. Pope Francis writes:

This is because fatherhood extends beyond simple procreation and biology. Fatherhood is first a spiritual reality, because fatherhood has its origins in God who chose to reveal himself to us as Our Father, sending his only Son for the sake of salvation. Fathers, therefore, have a special and unique role in "revealing and in reliving on earth the very fatherhood of God" (FC, 25). Fathers have a vital, unique, and important role to play in the personal and spiritual development of their children, and in reflecting the love of God the Father himself. Fathers are called to show the world the virtues of a tender protector, while living out the virtues of humility and courage.[29]

St. Francis DeSales

The second source of inspiration is attributed to one of the Doctors of the Church, St. Francis de Sales. St. Francis writes: "God takes pleasure to see you take your little steps; and like a good father who holds his child by the hand, He will accommodate His steps to yours and will be content to go no faster than you. Why do you worry?"

This quotation is worth unpacking. St. Francis reminds us that not only should we be patient with ourselves, but God is patient, too. He offers this beautiful image of a father holding the hand of a child. When you hold your child's hand, especially as they take their first steps, you will feel the primal urge to protect them and to also empower them to move forward. This resembles how our heavenly father is with us. God not only walks with us but supports us along this journey. Finally, St. Francis asks us, after telling us how God supports and accompanies us, "Why do you worry?"

In my eight-plus years of fatherhood, I know that my leading emotion has been love. Not far behind is that of worry. To this day, I put my hand on both my sleeping children's chests before I go to sleep to make sure they are breathing. When they were both babies, I would wake up throughout the night to do this as they slept next to us. Sometimes, I even woke them up to make sure they were all right. I don't blame them for reacting with a scowl or a scream. Even in writing this question posed some four hundred years ago, I struggle to find an answer to that why. Ultimately, I believe my worry is because of the depth of the love I have for my family. Only when I am in a place of prayer and silence am I reminded that this love comes from God; it is God, and that is why there is no reason to worry. Prayer becomes a consistent reminder of this truth—a truth that allows life to be one of peaceful presence.

Dorothy Day

As a New Yorker, I have a special love and admiration for Dorothy Day. For over a decade, I taught first-year students at St. John's University about Day, her life, and her impact, especially through the Catholic Worker.

What I love most about Day is how she was called to live the Gospel. It was by serving those most in need, especially those facing housing and food insecurity in Manhattan. She was also an advocate for human rights. Her life started with the great 1906 earthquake and 1908 fire in San Francisco. It was her mom's charity to those impacted that established a life-long lesson of charity and love for those in need. As a young adult in the early twentieth century, she advocated for a woman's right to vote, and near the end of her life, her advocacy focused on peace and anti-war efforts, especially against the Vietnam War.

Day was also a mom. She understood the pressures and responsibilities of having a child. Her grandchildren, all these years later, continue their grandmother's work as advocates and activists, standing up for human rights in all its forms.

Day said many wonderful things. I strongly recommend her book, *The Long Loneliness,* as an authentic and vulnerable witness of faith in action. There is also a 1996 film titled, *Entertaining Angels,* which tells the story of the early part of Day's life. Featuring actors Moira Kelly and Martin Sheen, it is a mostly historically accurate movie depicting this amazing life.

Day writes: "The greatest challenge of the day is how to bring about a revolution of the heart, a revolution which has to start with each one of us?"[30] As you look around and see such sad and depressing reports from your local, national, and global news sources, one can wonder, "Why would I bring a child into this world." The answer, of course, is love. There are countless examples of it, and who knows, your child may be a part of the revolution of love that transforms hurt to peace, war to peace, and hate to love. I like to believe that this revolution has already started before us, and continues with us, as it will with our children.

If your child learns to love God, self, neighbor, and stranger, then, these words of Day can begin to be fulfilled. As a Church, we look to St. Joseph and how his fatherhood prepared Jesus for his ministry. We do the same with St. Monica, the mother of St. Augustine. What if you are the parent to the next saint of the Church? If they have statues made in their image or not (it is never about this anyway), if they can live a life that is a revolution of the heart like Day says, then your life was extraordinary.

Day invites us, in this second quotation, to see beyond our immediate family and friend circles. It calls us to investigate and respond to those living on the margins of society. Attributed to Day is this saying, "I really only love God as much as I love the person I love the least."

As mentioned earlier, one of the greatest gifts I received was the opportunity to work at the United Nations, representing the Sisters of Charity Federation. My eyes have been painfully opened to the great injustices impacting our world. So many go without a healthy environment, clean water and food, fair wages, peaceful and stable housing, and non-violence. I ask myself, almost daily, how I can care so deeply for my girls and still have room in my heart and energy in my body to care for others who are less fortunate.

There are many populations in need. Perhaps, it is the children who offer the saddest testimony. As of 2022, 333 million children are living in extreme poverty (surviving on less than $2.15 per day).[31] Aren't these children our responsibility as fathers? I am not calling us to enter the scene with our capes on to save the day (this has never worked, by the way). Rather, I am asking us, as dads, to open our ears, eyes, and hearts. Learn more about the injustices on the local level. Then, look at our country and then the world.

Listen and understand instead of jumping to a judgment (enough people do this—and it only makes it worse). Ask, "How might I help," and follow up on the answer. We are not called to be dads only for our kids, our nephews and nieces, and our local schools and sports teams. Day urges us to look to the margins, those forgotten about or most impacted by injustice. What is ours to do? Or as St. Vincent de Paul was famously asked when he was overwhelmed by injustice, "What must be done."[32]

Chiara Lubich

In 1943, during the Second World War, with bombs flying overhead in Trent, Italy, Chiara Lubich, with her fellow young friends, turned to Scripture. The words, "[Father] that they may all be one" (John 17:21), turned into the foundation of the Focolare community seeking to unite all people. They knew there had to be another way to respond to war and the unnecessary loss and devastation. Lubich recalls when she and her companions reflected on this hope and mandate from Christ. Lubich writes, "This immediately led us to love everyone, without distinction, and to put ourselves at God's disposal, so that this testament of Jesus might be realized."[33]

Can we see fatherhood as a path to unity? Not just for our own home, but for God's home. Might we be called to contribute to this goal as fathers, men of faith, along with women and all of God's people? I believe this is our call to answer. As this small community found its direction, they went to the local bishop to see if they were doing God's will. The bishop exclaimed, "Here I see the hand of God."[34] Where do you see the hand of God today?

In my speaking engagements on fatherhood with Catholic communities, I am inspired by the movement of engaged fathers. In Western society, fatherhood meant provider, while nurturing and empathy belonged to mom. In recent decades, this has started to shift.

Even in popular culture, fictional television fathers like Homer Simpson, Al Bundy, and Tim "the Toolman" Taylor, among many others, depicted dads as silly, unreliable, and at times, causing more harm than good. Society told fathers that they had to provide for their family and told mothers that they had to take care of the home with little recognition and in many cases, work outside the home as well.

There is a shift occurring where dad and mom are finally seen as equal, although the pay gap does not currently reflect this. There are many cases where fathers assume the responsibilities of the home, and the pandemic accelerated the opportunity for dads to find the work-life balance and to be more present in the lives of their children. Shows like *Ted Lasso* and *Bluey* exemplify this, depicting fathers as being reliable, empathetic, and emotionally invested, along with mom, in the lives of their children.

A book like this calls us to see beyond our own homes, which is our first responsibility. There is a call to unity, and for fatherhood to not simply be equated with provider. Churches and faith communities need to establish space for men to be together, not to simply do, but to be. There is a clear yearning for a community of support as fatherhood is redefined. The hand of God is moving us forward and closer together as a people, despite the isolation and independence that technology enhances.

Lubich often writes that her communities sought to find "Jesus in their midst." Throughout this book, I exemplify this belief as often as I can, especially in the spirit of community where two or three are gathered in his name (Matt 18:20). Yes, this is meant for our little holy family, but it is also for our human holy family.

A shift in perspective, centered around God, allows us to move forward to a truer reality, united in unconditional love and support. Dads have a significant role to play in bringing this to fruition.

Saint Francis of Assisi

Often considered the most popular of saints, St. Francis of Assisi models the Christian life as a deep desire to replicate the love of Jesus. Francis has so many wonderful teachings and stories attributed to his life.

Attributed to Francis is the saying, "Start by doing what is necessary, then what is possible, and suddenly you are doing the impossible." This quotation is important as this book ends because it provides a roadmap for how to be a dad, a husband, a Christian, and for all our vocations. There will be moments when your cup is empty or when you are overwhelmed by the to-do lists, the uncontrollable, and the pain and suffering. You will look into a mirror filled with self-doubt and insecurity. Past and internal discouraging voices will creep in when you are at your most vulnerable.

Francis, who always calls us to a deep relationship with Christ, reminds us to begin by doing what is first necessary. Respond to the need in front of you. Then, explore what is possible. Begin to dream. Take chances. Follow the Holy Spirit nudging within your soul. Then, suddenly, you are doing what you thought not so long ago to be impossible.

Saint Vincent de Paul

St. Vincent de Paul writes: "God knows what is best for us, and He will give it to us at the right time if, like children who have perfect trust in such a good father, we abandon ourselves to Him." This is a call to trust our Father in Heaven who lives within us, our partner, our children, and all in our midst. Seek God in one another and seek God within. God is there, always.

I pray these pages helped you better appreciate this truth and prepared you for what is now your beautiful and blessed life. May God continue to bless you, your family, and your children. May God continue to transform your heart as a father and a husband. And may God continue to call you to be his good and faithful servant and son.

John O'Donohue

My favorite modern poet is John O'Donohue. He captures beauty in his connecting of words and thoughts, which leaves me inspired every time. I conclude this book with O'Donohue's poem, appropriately titled "For a New Father." I leave you with these words that serve as my final prayer for you:

As the shimmer of dawn transforms the night
Into a blush of color futured with delight,
The eyes of your new child awaken in you
A brightness that surprises your life.

Since the first stir of its secret becoming,
The echo of your child has lived inside you,
Strengthening through all its night of forming
Into a sure pulse of fostering music.

How quietly and gently that embryo-echo
Can womb in the bone of a man
And foster across the distance to the mother
A shadow-shelter around this fragile voyage.

Now as you behold your infant, you know
That this child has come from you and to you;
You feel the full force of a father's desire
To protect and shelter.

Perhaps for the first time,
There awakens in you
A sense of your own mortality.

May your heart rest in the grace of the gift
And you sense how you have been called
Inside the dream of this new destiny.

May you be gentle and loving,
Clear and sure.

May you trust in the unseen providence
That has chosen you all to be a family.

May you stand sure on our ground
And know that every grace you need
Will unfold before you
Like all the mornings of your life.[35]

Notes

1. Thomas Merton, *Choosing to Love the World: on Contemplation*, Jonathan Montaldo, ed. (Sounds True, 1st ed., 2008), 53. Kindle.
2. "Blessed Frederic Ozanam Biography," Vincentian Formation Network, November 11, 2013, http://vincentians.com/en/blessed-frederic-ozanam-biography-i/.
3. http://www.cultura.va/content/cultura/en/pub/documenti/ViaPulchritudinis.html.
4. https://www.vatican.va/content/francesco/en/apost_exhortations/documents/papa-francesco_esortazione-ap_20131124_evangelii-gaudium.html.
5. Henri J. M. Nouwen, quoted in "Life Is Precious," Henri Nouwen Society, October 19, 2023, https://henrinouwen.org/meditations/life-is-precious/.
6. Richard Rohr, "Love and Beauty," January 12, 2015, https://cac.org/daily-meditations/love-and-beauty-2015-01-12/.
7. Chiara Lubich, cited in Focolare.org, https://www.focolare.org/en/living-the-present-moment-well/.
8. Francis, *Patris Corde of the Holy Father Francis on the 150th Anniversary of the proclamation of Saint Joseph as Patron of the Universal Church* (December 8, 2020), 7, Apostolic Letter, https://www.vatican.va/content/francesco/en/apost_letters/documents/papa-francesco-lettera-ap_20201208_patris-corde.html.
9. Mother Teresa, as cited in "Acceptance Speech," The Nobel Prize, April 9, 2024, https://www.nobelprize.org/prizes/peace/1979/teresa/acceptance-speech/.
10. Meister Eckhart, from *Meister Eckhart's Book of Secrets: Meditations on Letting Go and Finding True Freedom*, translated by Mark S. Burrows and Jon M. Sweeney (Hampton Roads Publishing Company, 2019).
11. Dorothy Day, as cited in "Dorothy Day," Holy Hill Hermitage, https://www.holyhill.ie/dorothy-day/.
12. Henri J. M. Nouwen, *The Inner Voice of Love: A Journey Through Anguish to Freedom* (Image, 1996).

13. Francis, General Audience. February 11, 2015, https://www.vatican.va/content/francesco/en/audiences/2015/documents/papa-francesco_20150211_udienza-generale.html.
14. https://poets.org/poem/children-1.
15. St. Peter Julian Eymard, as cited in "Saint Quotes About St. Joseph," Year of Saint Joseph, https://yearofstjoseph.org/quotes/#:~:text=St.-Peter%20Julian%20Eymard,were%20committed%20to%20his%20care.
16. Richard Wagamese, *Embers: One Ojibway's Meditations* (Douglas and McIntyre, 2016). Ebook.
17. Francis, as cited in https://www.bbcatholic.org.au/north-harbour/news-events/pastors-perspective/pastor-s-perspective-the-names-of-our-fathers. Accessed May 2, 2024.
18. "Just to See You Smile," written by Mark Nesler and Tony Martin.
19. https://time.com/archive/6703981/interview-with-mother-teresa-a-pencil-in-the-hand-of-god/.
20. Thomas Merton, *Love and Living*, edited by Naomi Burton Stone and Patrick Hart, (Harcourt, Inc., 1981), 27.
21. Elizabeth Anne Seton and Robert Seton, *Memoir, Letters and Journal of Elizabeth Seton*, edited by R. Seton (United States, n.p, 1869), 82.
22. Francis, General Audience, February 4, 2015, https://www.vatican.va/content/francesco/en/audiences/2015/documents/papa-francesco_20150204_udienza-generale.html#:~:text=Every%20family%20needs%20a%20father,heart%20too%20will%20be%20glad.
23. Siobhan Quenby, et al., "Miscarriage matters: the epidemiological, physical, psychological, and economic costs of early pregnancy loss," *Lancet*. May 1, 2021.
24. Cited in https://www.savethechildren.org/us/what-we-do/health/newborn-health#:~:text=The%20first%2028%20days%20of,globally%20during%20pregnancy%20or%20childbirth.
25. Geraldine Guadagno, *John of the Smiles* (New City Press, 2016).
26. https://www.newmanreader.org/works/meditations/meditations9.html.
27. https://www.ssvpglobal.org/where-we-are/.
28. http://vincentians.com/en/quotes-collection/frederic-ozanam-quotes/.
29. Francis, *Patris Corde*.

30. Dorothy Day, *Loaves and Fishes* (Orbis Books, 1997).
31. United Nations, https://www.unicef.org/social-policy/child-poverty.
32. Cited by John Freund, in FamVin 2024: The Vincentian Questions- What Must Be Done?
33. Chiara Lubich, *May They All Be One: Origins and Life of the Focolare Movement*, revised edition (New City Press, 2023), 22.
34. Lubich, *May They All Be One*, 23.
35. John O'Donohue, *To Bless the Space Between Us: A Book of Blessings*. Cited in http://mollystrongheart.blogspot.com/2015/02/john-odonohue-for-new-father.html.

Sources Consulted

Burrows, Mark S. and Sweeney, Jon M., translators. *Meister Eckhart's Book of Secrets: Meditations on Letting Go and Finding True Freedom.* Charlottesville: Hampton Roads Publishing Company, 2019.

Day, Dorothy. "Dorothy Day." n.d. *Holy Hill Hermitage.* Accessed May 1, 2024. https://www.holyhill.ie/dorothy- day/.

Day, Dorothy. *Loaves and Fishes.* Orbis Books, 1997.

Dicastery of Culture and Education. The *Via Pulchritudinis*, Way of Beauty. http://www.cultura.va/content/cultura/en/pub/documenti/ViaPulchritudinis.html. Accessed May 17, 2024.

Francis. *Evangelii Gaudium* [The Joy of the Gospel], 2013. https://www.vatican.va/content/francesco/en/apost_exhortations/documents/papa-francesco_esortazione-ap_20131124_evangelii-gaudium.html.

Francis. General Audience, February 4, 2015. https://www.vatican.va/content/francesco/en/audiences/2015/documents/papa-francesco_20150204_udienza-generale.html#:~:text=Every%20family%20needs%20a%20father,heart%20too%20will%20be%20glad.

Francis. General Audience, February 11, 2015. https://www.vatican.va/content/francesco/en/audiences/2015/documents/papa-francesco_20150211_udienza-generale.html.

Francis. Apostolic Letter, *Patris Corde of the Holy Father Francis On the 150th Anniversary of the Proclamation of Saint Joseph as Patron of the Universal Church*, December 8, 2020. https://www.vatican.va/content/francesco/en/apost_letters/documents/papa-francesco-lettera-ap_20201208_patris-corde.html.

Freund, John, "The Vincentian Questions- What Must Be Done?" The Vincentian Family Information Network, in *FamVin 2024.* https://famvin.org/en/2018/01/27/vincentian-question-must-done/.

Guadagno, Geraldine, *John of the Smiles.* New City Press. 2016.

Henri J. M. Nouwen. "Life Is Precious." *Henri Nouwen Society.* October 19, 2023. https://henrinouwen.org/meditations/life-is-precious/.

Lubich, Chiara. *May They All Be One: Origins and Life of the Focolare Movement*, revised edition. New City Press, 2023.

Lubich, Chiara. Cited in Focolare.org. https://www.focolare.org/en/living-the-present-moment-well/. Accessed April 28, 2024.

Merton, Thomas, *Choosing to Love the World: On Contemplation*. Edited by Jonathan Montaldo. Sounds True, 1st edition, 2008. Kindle.

Merton, Thomas. *Love and Living*. Edited by Naomi Burton Stone and Patrick Hart. Harcourt. 1981.

Newman, John Henry. https://www.newmanreader.org/works/meditations/meditations9.html.

Nouwen, Henri J. M. *The Inner Voice of Love: A Journey Through Anguish to Freedom*. Image. 1996.

O'Donohue, John. "For a New Father." *Molly Strongheart Blogspot*. February 27, 2015. https://mollystrongheart.blogspot.com/2015/02/john-odonohue-for-new- father.html.

Quenby, Siobhan, et al. "Miscarriage matters: the epidemiological, physical, psychological, and economic costs of early pregnancy loss." *Lancet*. May 1, 2021. 397(10285):1658-1667. doi: 10.1016/S0140-6736(21)00682-6. Epub 2021 Apr 27. PMID: 33915094. https://pubmed.ncbi.nlm.nih.gov/33915094/#:~:text=Miscarriage%20is%20generally%20defined%20as,%25)%20of%20all%20recognised%20pregnancies.

Rohr, Richard. "Love and Beauty." *Center for Action and Contemplation*. January 12, 2015. https://cac.org/daily-meditations/love-and-beauty-2015-01-12/.

Save the Children. Accessed May 1, 2024. https://www.savethechildren.org/us/what-we-do/health/newborn-health#:~:text=The%20first%2028%20days%20of,globally%20during%20pregnancy%20or%20childbirth.

Seton, Elizabeth Anne, and Robert Seton. *Memoir, Letters and Journal of Elizabeth Seton*. Edited by R. Seton. United States. n. p. 1869.

Teresa. *Nobel Peace Prize*. "Acceptance Speech." April 9, 2024. https://www.nobelprize.org/prizes/peace/1979/teresa/acceptance-speech/.

The Catholic Community of North Harbour, n.d., "Pastor's Perspective—'The Names of our Fathers,' https://www.bbcatholic.org.au/north-harbour/news-events/pastors-perspective/pastor-s-perspective-the-names-of-our-fathers. Accessed May 2, 2024.

United Nations, https://www.unicef.org/social-policy/child-poverty. Accessed May 3, 2024.

Vincentians.com. "Quotes-Frederic Ozanam." http://vincentians. com/en/quotes- collection/frederic-ozanam-quotes/. Accessed May 3, 2024.

Wagamese, Richard. *Embers: One Ojibway's Meditations*. Douglas and McIntyre, 2016. Ebook.

Year of St. Joseph. "Saint Quotes About St. Joseph." https://yearofstjoseph. org/quotes/#:~:text=St.,Peter%20Julian%20Eymard,were%20 committed%20to%20his%20care." Accessed May 3, 2024.

FOCOLARE MEDIA
Enkindling the Spirit of Unity

The New City Press book you are holding in your hands is one of the many resources produced by Focolare Media, which is a ministry of the Focolare Movement in North America. The Focolare is a worldwide community of people who feel called to bring about the realization of Jesus' prayer: "That all may be one" (see John 17:21).

Focolare Media wants to be your primary resource for connecting with people, ideas, and practices that build unity. Our mission is to provide content that empowers people to grow spiritually, improve relationships, engage in dialogue, and foster collaboration within the Church and throughout society.

 Visit www.focolaremedia.com to learn more about all of New City Press's books, our award-winning magazine *Living City*, videos, podcasts, events, and free resources.

NEW CITY PRESS

www.ingramcontent.com/pod-product-compliance
Lightning Source LLC
Chambersburg PA
CBHW071721090426
42738CB00009B/1837